Damaged Language

Radio Plays
by
Richard Nelson

BROADWAY PLAY PUBLISHING INC
New York
www.broadwayplaypublishing.com
info@broadwayplaypublishing.com

Introduction
© Copyright 2019 Ned Chaillet
Damaged Language
© Copyright 2019 Richard Nelson

All rights reserved. This work is fully protected under the copyright laws of the United States of America. No part of this publication may be photocopied, reproduced, stored in a retrieval system, or transmitted, in any form or by any means, electronic, mechanical, recording, or otherwise, without the prior permission of the publisher. Additional copies of this play are available from the publisher.

Written permission is required for live performance of any sort. This includes readings, cuttings, scenes, and excerpts. For amateur and stock performances, please contact Broadway Play Publishing Inc. For all other rights please contact Patrick Herold, I C M, pherold@icmpartners.com.

First edition: January 2019
I S B N: 978-0-88145-821-3

Book design: Marie Donovan
Page make-up: Adobe InDesign
Typeface: Palatino

Introduction by Ned Chaillet .... *v*
LANGUAGES SPOKEN HERE 1
EATING WORDS 53
ADVICE TO EASTERN EUROPE 101
THE AMERICAN WIFE 143

EVERY WORD COUNTS

Richard Nelson Radio Plays

Ned Chaillet

Introduction

Between 1987 and 2009 Richard Nelson wrote six play for B B C radio. *Roots in Water*, broadcast in 1989 on B B C Radio 3, was subtitled "Twelve Scenes from an American Generation" and was an expanded version of an intimate yet epic sequence of short stage plays that captured individual Americans in the ripples that spread out from the Vietnam war from 1976 to 1988, the eras of presidents Jimmy Carter and Ronald Reagan.

Hyde Park-on-Hudson, broadcast on Radio 3 in 2009, concerned a visit by England's King George VI and Queen Elizabeth (later the Queen Mother) to President Franklin D Roosevelt's home on the Hudson River in 1939. As viewed by Roosevelt's distant cousin and companion, Margaret "Daisy" Suckley—depicted with some controversy as F D R's secret lover—the play contrasted the most intimate details of Daisy's relationship with the president to the gathering storm that was the impending war with Germany.

Like much of Richard's stage work, *Hyde Park-on-Hudson* has its roots in Rhinebeck, New York, where Richard lives and where Stuckley died in 1991. Using the journals discovered after her death, Richard captured a pivotal historic event through often comic domestic detail.

On radio, F D R was played by Tim Piggott-Smith, with Emma Fielding as Daisy. When the movie version was made in 2012, directed by Roger Michell, F D R was played by Bill Murray, with Laura Linney as Daisy.

The B B C, it might be noted, had a problem with the depiction of Queen Elizabeth. A commissioning editor said she had been taught that the B B C had a duty of care to the Royal Family and depicting Queen Elizabeth drinking alcohol and smoking, which she did, was possibly unnecessary. The Queen Mother had died, aged 101, in 2002.

The four other plays, conceived for radio, were shorter, succinct dramas (including a blatant comedy) of the aural imagination. Almost nothing written for radio is immune to life in another medium, as words are most carefully honed in good radio. Tom Stoppard lamented when his most radio-phonic play, *Artist Descending A Staircase*, had a successful stage life years after the radio production. "Another failure", he said.

Nelson's plays for radio are journeys for the ear. They are not immune to visualization, because listeners paint their own pictures. We encounter misunderstandings across different languages and in the same language; we roll through London parks and hear the creak of bedsprings to the accompaniment of a radio reading of a book at bedtime. We also go into the love struck thoughts of a besotted script reader, and into the inner thoughts of a distracted wife in her last

Introduction   vii

month of pregnancy, when the very words and sounds we are hearing are unreliable.

For a writer whose craft as a wordsmith is regularly honored, the shop floor of dramatic speech, as it was for writers such as Stoppard, Harold Pinter, Caryl Churchill and Arthur Miller, was radio. What you learn from the radio plays of Richard Nelson is that every word counts.

LANGUAGES SPOKEN HERE

When I first met Richard Nelson, at an awards ceremony in London when his play *Principia Scriptoriae* was one of the successes for the Royal Shakespeare Company season at London's Barbican Theatre, I asked him if he had thought of writing for the radio. He had, and had recently sent a script to the B B C's Radio Drama department. As I was editor of Radio 3 plays, I went back to Broadcasting House and had a search for the play. Submissions were well organized at the time and I took it from the stacks of scripts with a play reader.

The play was called LANGUAGES SPOKEN HERE and featured a displaced American translator, Michael Milick, who was meeting a Polish writer exiled in London to discuss translating one of his novels into English. Janusz Vukovski was certain of the value of his work, even if Michael had reservations and, it transpired, misunderstandings of the book's intentions. For Michael, the act of translating the book was part charity and in part for the experience of refreshing his Polish. For Janusz it was necessary, for both establishing his reputation in English, and financially.

There are early warning signs for the linguist Michael that he might be out of his depth. Michael proclaims that he is Polish, even though he is from the American mid-West and his specialist language is German, and he stumbles at the very beginning by insisting that book's title, literally "The Hairpiece" should be called "The Bald Spot" in English.

Janusz remarks: "Our minister of defense wears a hairpiece. In Poland, in Warsaw, you say hairpiece, and everyone thinks minister of defense. I don't suppose you do here."

It takes a moment, but Michael finally asks: "You mean it's a reference, then, the title, to the Polish minister of defense?"

There will be a lot that Michael, the Pole from Michigan, doesn't get.

Set in 1987, the year the play was written, it is a world in which Eastern Europe and the West were firmly divided by ideology and Cold War borders. The borders between people are less visible at first. Touched by the difficulties Janusz faces in bringing his family out of Poland, Michael and his wife offer him meals, a chair for his cramped bed-sit, the loan of a family cottage and friendship, but misunderstand Janusz's needs.

"All I do know is that being nice and doing favors has nothing to do with writing books or making art. Being nice and doing favors is what one does between writing books and making art." is the Pole's understanding of their relationship.

Richard Nelson is an exceptionally precise writer. His ear for the rhythms of speech is a gift to the actor, and to radio. Carefully chosen words are just part of a conversation: hesitations are often naturally funny, but they can also lay trip-wires of misdirection, allowing characters to hide behind a pause.

Introduction   ix

To an actor such as Colin Stinton, Canada-born and Chicago-trained who took the part of Michael, Nelson's dialogue is a gymnasium of expression. An intended joke can flip into embarrassed self-realization and an expression of gentle disappointment can turn into a drop of acid. The carefully chosen English of Janusz, loaded with a mocking irony, allowed the actor Renny Krupinski a severe playfulness that Michael would do well to notice.

In the recording of the play the Czechoslovakian actor playing Janusz's friend—it was still Czechoslovakia in 1987—gave a resonant demonstration of the simple linguistic pitfalls of a single word. Totally comfortable with the text, he came to a halt with the stage direction "beat". Jiri Hanak was expecting the drum strike he would have expected in Prague. Nelson's script was simply calling for a break in rhythm, the "slight pause" Harold Pinter would write for his actors.

LANGUAGES SPOKEN HERE went on to win a Giles Cooper Award for Best Radio Plays of 1987, an award honoring the prolific radio writer Giles Cooper—his stage play *Everything in the Garden* was adapted by Edward Albee in the United Starts—and sponsored by the publishers Methuen and the B B C.

EATING WORDS

Edward Asner was in London, filming a Jeffrey Archer mini-series, when Richard Nelson gave me his latest radio play, EATING WORDS. At the center of the play were two old friends, very different novelists who usually met twice a year for uninhibited lunches where, with wine and whiskey, they bared the emotional content behind their latest publications. Henry, an English writer who had pioneered a confessional path in gay fiction, struck me as a character who would benefit from the weight of a Royal Shakespeare Company actor such as John Woodvine, adept at linguistic complexities and delighting in the delicacies of Richard's playful and cautiously revealing emotional truths.

His friend, the boisterous and bumptious American novelist Sam, was harder to find in the pool of Americans in England. Sam's latest novel had caused uproar in his family, with his English wife, an actress, decamping the family home for her perceived depiction in the book. His shameless exploitation of friends and family for commercial success did not prevent him from feeling guilt over his failure to use his talent to make a difference in America in the era of President Ronald Reagan. (Philip Roth, it transpires in the play, is said to like the new book.)

I had heard Ed Asner's fine and skillful performances in audio for L.A. Theatre Works productions, and the intelligence, humor and lucidity of his television work as Lou Grant and others made him the perfect actor for Sam, so, with Richard's approval, I wrote a cover letter, packaged up a copy of the script, and took it to the London Hilton in Park Lane, where Asner was staying.

On the Saturday, when he returned from filming, I got a phone call at home. He said, "This is Ed Asner. I'm halfway through the script and want to do it. Here are my available dates."

We found dates when a studio was available, and, with even more luck, when John Woodvine was available. The two actors, one so finely English and the other so openly American, immediately found a history of performance that felt like a friendship of decades. As so often in Richard's writing, despite the uninhibited and openly confessional revelations of the characters—Henry's grief at the loss of his lover is raw

Introduction

in its pain, but the ongoing plague of 1989 is unspoken. It is delicately revealed that Henry is in a wheelchair at their lunch, but it is not long before the friends are challenging the streets and parks of London, roaring through crowds.

Once again, the year matters. The stories happen in a real world, with history pressing at the personal dramas and comedies of his characters. While Sam has a pressing story to tell about his marriage crumbling because of the revelations of his latest novel, Henry's more hesitant telling about the cost to his relationship of his last novel, to his last lover, is even more intense. But this is not a cloistered drinking session, rather it moves, partly fuelled by alcohol, in a world full of people, almost hallucinatory at times as Sam and Henry trigger a tirade from a young English woman raging in her praise of the new America that has brought Sam into loud despair.

The play demands an ensemble of unnamed people filling the space around the two friends, from the young woman raging in a pub to the drinkers roaring their approval, to the crowds blocking the progress of the wheelchair as Sam and Henry roll through their confessions, and fantasies. Henry will never take the lecturing job on offer in America, once his condition is seen; Sam will exploit the intimate details of his life, and not step on to the political stage with his writing.

To record this journey, Woodvine was strapped into a wheelchair, with a microphone mounted above his head on a suspended ball while a studio manager presented the script to Asner, who was pushing the wheelchair through moving crowds of actors as another microphone picked up the people and the space they moved in. Asner pushed the wheelchair in a figure eight round and round the actors, carefully treading above the snake-like cables beneath their feet.

"Usually, when I do this in America", said Asner, "We sit at a table with a microphone." His whole physical commitment to the play was driven by the script.

The play was broadcast in Britain and across the world as part of B B C World Service collaboration. It won Nelson a second Giles Cooper Award.

ADVICE TO EASTERN EUROPE

The distance from London to Prague is 642 miles; from London to Moscow, 1,554 miles. New York City is 3, 466 miles from London, but despite the tilted geographical toward Eastern Europe, Richard Nelson's plays regularly put London at the epicentre of the East/West divide.

ADVICE TO EASTERN EUROPE is a comedy set at that epicentre of misunderstandings in 1990, just a year after the Berlin Wall was opened up and as its slow demolition was underway, and a year after the "Velvet Revolution" in Czechoslovakia, that gentle uprising which saw the end of 40 years of communist rule and marked a time of great optimism, with some triumphalism in the West.

Nelson's gently velvet comedy focuses on a young Czech screenwriter, Helena, whose loveliness so transfixes Paul, an American script editor, that he can barely follow the conversation as she pitches projects to a London film company.

Paul remains transfixed, but gradually manages to communicate, escorting Helena to a media watering-hole, seeing off the advances of a lecherous lecturer and succumbing to the bookshop and operatic enthusiasms of Helena in her last night in London. (*Katya Kabionva*, an "opera in Czech!")

Introduction   xiii

Helena, for her part, never loses sight of the reason she is there. Her father, a famous filmmaker admired by Paul, has seized on the rapid political changes to look out from Czechoslovakia. "It was he," she says, "who sent me to London to see, now that there is freedom and democracy in my country, what projects the West might be interested in."

Paul, so disillusioned with the politics in his own country, cannot refrain from criticizing Helena's optimistic vision of the West. A favorite project of hers, which would transfer the dreams of Chekhov's provincial *Three Sisters* who yearn for Moscow to an actual move to New York City while fleeing war in Europe, is initially scorned.

Her idea that New York can symbolize hope rankles as does her suggestion that the characters would remain faithful to their nature, that "If we are bad people living in a hell, we will also be bad people living in a heaven".

"Heaven!", Paul exclaims, "… I think, as an American, that the country is living one great big lie."

Paul's attempts to deflate Helena's expectations of the West seem, for a moment, set to derail a growing mutual attraction—it is, perhaps, not advisable to advise an eastern European on the limits of freedom in 1990.

1990, that febrile year, is marvelously captured in Nelson's writing. *Time Out*, the London listings magazine is still the city's cultural guide, and you still had to pay for it. Dillon's Bookshop in Covent Garden was open late (due, as Paul notes, to Margaret Thatcher's cuts, which led to the closure of the Arts Council bookshop on the site. Thatcher would resign in November 1990.) It allowed Helena to buy a copy of

TTHREE SISTERS in English, and later, in the streets, a busker would sing, "Bridge over Troubled Water".

(ADVICE TO EASTERN EUROPE is an early statement of intent as far as Chekhov is concerned. Nelson's adaptation of THREE SISTERS would be seen at Chicago's Goodman Theater in 1995. His versions of THE CHERRY ORCHARD, THE SEAGULL and UNCLE VANYA in collaboration with the translators Richard Pevear and Larissa Volokhonsky resonate in the 21st century.)

While Nelson's first two radio plays, LANGUAGES SPOKEN HERE and EATING WORDS, offered cool, slightly distanced frames in which to observe the action, in a manner which might have appealed to Bertolt Brecht, ADVICE TO EASTERN EUROPE goes straight into the interior of Paul's thoughts and emotions only gradually pulling back so we can witness an argument in a restaurant, a rain-soaked dash through the streets to Helena's hotel and a climactic squeak of bedsprings accompanied by a radio reading E M Forster's *A Room with a View* on a book at bedtime.

Comedy of this subtlety requires chemistry, and the Czechoslovakia-born English actress Edita Brychta brought charm and a wise knowingness to the role of Helena. Her cinematic sweetness, seductive and rich in experience that suggested the fall of more than a political wall, sparked a surprisingly vulnerable and funny performance from Colin Stinton, an actor richly attuned to Paul's slow capitulation to the East, when Prague seems more desirable than his past.

THE AMERICAN WIFE

Thursday is "a stupid day to have a holiday" according to Anne's husband, Harry. "Why can't we have Thanksgiving on Saturday or Sunday?"

Introduction   xv

It may be a stupid day to the Englishman Harry, but, for Anne, in her eighth month of pregnancy and third year in London, a Thanksgiving dinner is a slightly desperate way to bring America to England. As she tells us, after three years she wants to go home.

Harry leaves it to Anne to persuade their friends, Fiona and John, to take time off to join them at lunchtime on a Thursday for the American holiday. Fiona, a publisher, even finds a visiting American novelist to bring along:

"She said he wasn't an important author, so why not?", says Anne.

It is always Anne speaking to us, drifting in and out of the dinner table conversation about gardens, holidays and children while being reminded by the American guest of her first love and graphically reliving their sexual fumbling.

Sex was already on her mind as she listens in on her husband's intimate calls with his lover, counts his condoms and marks his underpants with her initial to prove that he is secretly changing his underwear during the day. There is a problem with Anne's own reliability, however. She is sometimes certain that she has spoken aloud, only for no one but the radio listener to hear her, and then, what is meant as an inner thought is spoken aloud.

For THE AMERICAN WIFE, first heard on B B C Radio 4 in 1996, Richard Nelson had the unusual luxury of writing the play for a special actor and the subtle, anguished and comic lines are perfectly tailored to the gifts of Zoë Wanamaker. Strictly speaking, although she was born in New York City in 1948, Zoë was not quite an American import like Anne. She had arrived in England as a small child with her actor father and mother and stayed in England when it became clear that her father, Sam Wanamaker, would be summoned by the House Un-American Activities Committee if they returned to the States at the height of the McCarthy era "witch hunt" in 1952.

Zoë, like Richard Nelson, had a long association with the Royal Shakespeare Company. For the company she shone in Shakespeare and won an Olivier Award for the R S C's revival of Kaufman and Hart's American classic ONCE IN A LIFETIME. Her performance in THE AMERICAN WIFE shows the classical control that the play demands as the listener is offered conflicting versions of events.

What you hear is sometimes what Anne thinks she hears, but at times it is what she does not hear as she rummages in her thoughts and suspicions. There is a mystery about her, even as she seizes on the 30-minute play like an unreliable Hitchcock blonde while Anton Lesser as her husband belligerently protests his innocence, or is a manipulative man out of *Gaslight*.

For all that Nelson's keen ear for one of Zoë Wanamaker's many voices is pitch perfect and puts her at the center of the play, it is finally an ensemble piece where the actors build the world around her. The conversations and phrases that drift through Anne's inner turmoil are finely attuned to the English and American voices that come from both her past and present. For Anne, it is the suspicious underpants of her husband; for Fiona pregnancy is preggers.

Listeners to the original B B C production will find one universe of dramatically connected actors, but readers may find that their own alternative universe can emerge, when the personal rendering of Zoe Wanamaker's Anne may tilt in another direction. Harry attributes his wife's moods to her hormones, but the theatre critic Michael Billington's review of the

Introduction   xvii

radio production for *The Guardian* sees the play's sharp contrasts between Anne's isolation and the country she is living in as something more culturally significant. He describes the play "a reminder that Nelson is the sharpest observer around of the gulf separating Britain and America."

October, 2018

Ned Chaillet delivered The Washington Post *as a boy in Washington, DC, was a copywriter on the* Washington Evening Star, *a sub-editor on* The Times Literary Supplement, *a theatre critic for* The Times *(London) and* The Wall Street Journal-Europe *and was an editor, producer and director for B B C Radio Drama. He lives in Herefordshire, England.*

LANGUAGES SPOKEN HERE

LANGUAGES SPOKEN HERE was first broadcast on BBC Radio 3 on 11 December 1987. The cast was as follows:

MICHAEL MILICK	Colin Stinton
ANNIE MILICK	Emily Richard
JANUSZ VUKOVSKI	Renny Krupinski
JAN KOSKTA	Jiri Hanak
ANDREW	Peter Craze
GEORGE SIMPSON	Steven Harrold
PETER MACK	John Samson
JANE	Karen Archer
Director	Ned Chaillet

CHARACTERS & SETTING

MICHAEL MILICK, *late thirties, American, translator from German and now Polish.*

ANNIE MILICK, *thirties, British,* MICHAEL's *wife and assistant to Carol Howard,* MICHAEL's *literary agent.*

JANUSZ VUKOSOVIC, *fifties, Polish, novelist and playwright.*

JAN KOSKTA, *early forties, Czech writer, he speaks no English.*

ANDREW, *thirties, producer of a small theater, British.*

GEORGE SIMPSON, *thirties, British, involved in publishing.*

PETER MACK, *forties, British, involved in publishing.*

JANE, *thirties, British, involved in publishing.*

Time & place: Today, London.

1.
Michael and Janusz meet.

(Interior. JANUSZ's flat. Morning)

(Door buzzer. JANUSZ's footsteps as he goes to the door. He opens the door.)

MICHAEL: Mr Vukosovic?

JANUSZ: Yes.

(Short pause)

MICHAEL: Mr Janusz Vukosovic?

JANUSZ: What do you want?

MICHAEL: Michael. Michael Milick.

JANUSZ: Yes. *(Beat)* I thought you said nine. Come in.

(Footsteps)

MICHAEL: No, ten. I even wrote down "ten". You haven't been waiting since nine, I hope, Mr Vuk—.

JANUSZ: Janusz. Call me Janusz. *(Beat)* This is the West after all. How do you do?

MICHAEL: I'm sure we said—

JANUSZ: Some tea?

MICHAEL: I'm never late. I'm practically famous for never being—

JANUSZ: Or is it coffee?

(Short pause)

MICHAEL: Tea. *(Beat)* If it's no trouble.

JANUSZ: Why should tea by trouble? *(Beat)* I have a kettle. *(He turns on the tap and fills the kettle. as he fills it:)* The first object I buy. I also have biscuits. And I am soon going to buy also a little cart to pull my groceries in. *(Finishes with the tap)* There is not much more to being British that I can see. Don't you agree?

MICHAEL: I don't know. I'm American.

JANUSZ: This I know. *(Beat)* It was my thought that you and I could make jokes of the British together. *(Beat)* When I am with a British person, we have no problem making fun of the Americans. *(Beat)* Did you know this?

MICHAEL: I'm not surprised.

(Beat)

JANUSZ: What I do not understand though is why when the Americans and the British get together you never make jokes about the Polish. *(Beat)* You never do this, do you? *(Beat)* I have been told this many many times.

MICHAEL: *(Laughs to himself)* To be honest...

JANUSZ: Please don't tell me this isn't the truth. I could not bear to think I have been lied to by my new friends. I put so much trust in them. *(Beat)* I have no choice but to trust them. *(Beat)* And that is the only way to trust. When you have no choice. Don't you agree?

(After a short pause:)

MICHAEL: I don't know.

JANUSZ: Please, eat a biscuit. I bought them for you. *(Short pause)* Take another one. *(Beat)* Take a third one.

MICHAEL: *(With his mouth full)* No, thank you.

JANUSZ: This morning, at the Sainsbury's—and what a shop that is; the size!

MICHAEL: *(Mouth full)* By American standards—.

JANUSZ: I was there buying these biscuits to have for you, and I say to myself—this Mr Milick—.

MICHAEL: *(Mouth full)* Michael.

JANUSZ: Michael. *(Beat)* Thank you, Michael. Thank you. *(Beat)* I want him—you—to like me. Not only my novel which I know he will like— *(Beat)* And want to translate. *(Beat)* But also me. *(Laughs)* Two months in the West and already I am full of anxieties. *(Laughs. Pause)* So I think I shall bribe you with biscuits. But you are not bribed, are you?

MICHAEL: I don't think so.

JANUSZ: Then allow me to tell you how very lucky I am to have caught your attention, Michael. Everyone has told me this. Everyone speaks like this about you.

MICHAEL: I'm flattered.

JANUSZ: This is the intention. *(Pause)* You have not read my book?

MICHAEL: No. But I assumed—or presumed—that this was one of the reasons for my coming by. *(Beat)* To pick up a copy.

JANUSZ: In Poland it is a very well-known book.

MICHAEL: I understand that. I'm eager to read it.

JANUSZ: Not that there aren't better books. Two of my books are better than this. *(Beat)* And three of my plays. I have plays as well. *(Short pause)* Successful plays.

(Kettle boils.)

JANUSZ: There is your tea.

MICHAEL: You're not having any?

(Kettle stops boiling.)

JANUSZ: Sit down, please. This is the comfortable chair. This one is not broken yet. *(As he serves the tea:)*

I suppose it wouldn't take long to read the book. It is rather a short book.

MICHAEL: I plan to read it right away.

JANUSZ: One could read it in one night, I suppose.

(Short pause)

MICHAEL: I couldn't tonight. *(Beat)* If that's what you're...

JANUSZ: Milk?

MICHAEL: Yes. *(Short pause)* I'm busy tonight. Maybe tomorrow though. *(Beat)* Tomorrow isn't too late, is it?

JANUSZ: Tomorrow? No. *(Beat)* Why would tomorrow be too late? Ten o'clock wasn't too late.

MICHAEL: Really, I'm pretty positive I said—.

JANUSZ: Nine. Ten. Today. Tomorrow. *(Beat)* Next year. *(Beat)* So I wait. I have nothing else to do. *(Beat)* I'm not the one who is busy. *(Beat)* What are you doing tonight that makes you so busy?

MICHAEL: A meeting. *(Beat)* A party. *(Beat)* With a lot of publishing types.

JANUSZ: That is important for a translator? To be with publishing types?

MICHAEL: I'm told so.

(Short pause)

JANUSZ: And for writers too it must be a good thing— to meet publishing types. *(Beat)* No?

MICHAEL: Yes. I would think so.

JANUSZ: I have met very few people here. Is there a special purpose for this party?

MICHAEL: No purpose. Just to get together. *(Beat)* And talk. *(Beat)* Put faces to names. *(Short pause)* Janusz I'd ask you to come along, but I hardly know the other—.

JANUSZ: I would be in the way.

MICHAEL: No, it's not—.

JANUSZ: I wasn't asking to come.

MICHAEL: I know you weren't, but—.

JANUSZ: Anyway, I see my friend, Jan Kostka, tonight. *(Beat)* You know my friend, Jan Kostka?

MICHAEL: No. I don't think I—.

JANUSZ: We get together and praise each other's books. He loves my books. I didn't think a Czech would like them so much. *(Beat)* His books are not so good. But I don't tell him, of course. *(Short pause)* He is a very good friend. He visited me once in Warsaw. He saw what I big flat I had there. *(Pause)* Where did you study Polish?

MICHAEL: I am Polish. Didn't my agent tell you?

JANUSZ: *(In Polish:)* From where?

MICHAEL: *(In English:)* Hamtramack, Michigan.

JANUSZ: *(In Polish:)* Where?

MICHAEL: *(In English:)* Michigan. That's in the Mid-West. It's a state. *(Beat)* Some of it is very Polish. *(Beat)* There's even a Mass in Polish in Hamtramack. *(Short pause)* I took my degree though in German. And it's mostly German that I—.

JANUSZ: *(In Polish:)* How's the tea?

MICHAEL: *(In English:)* The tea is fine, thank you.

(Short pause)

JANUSZ: *(In Polish:)* Another biscuit, Michael?

MICHAEL: *(In English:)* Two biscuits are plenty, thanks. *(Short pause)* If this is a test, I do read it quite fluently. *(Pause)* Though I've mostly translated from the German.

JANUSZ: Yes?

MICHAEL: Let me give you a list of my titles. Here's a list. There.

(Short pause)

JANUSZ: Well.

MICHAEL: Didn't my agent give you the list?

JANUSZ: Yes. *(Beat)* Yes, she did. *(Chews a biscuit:)* I cannot wait to know what you think of my book, Michael. I shall be so interested to talk to you about it. *(Beat)* Someone who knows Polish. Someone who is— "Polish". This is very exciting for me. *(Short pause)* Tomorrow morning I shall sit myself down next to that phone, Michael.

MICHAEL: Janusz—

JANUSZ: First thing in the morning, I shall do this.

MICHAEL: Now you know I may not even get to it until the early afternoon.

JANUSZ: Michael, I have nothing else to do. *(Beat)* Nothing. What do I have to do? *(Beat)* But wait for you.

(Fade out)

2.
Learning To Play.

(A flat in Islington. Early evening)

(A party is going on; loud talk, music, etc.)

GEORGE: *(Over the music)* Michael, would you be a dear and reach me one of those white wines? *(Beat)* Thanks. *(Beat)* You're not drinking?

MICHAEL: I have reading to do tonight.

GEORGE: You are conscientious.

MICHAEL: That's why I can't stay—.

JANE: George, is that you?

GEORGE: Jane.

JANE: Have you two met?

PETER: I don't believe—

JANE: Peter Mack, George Simpson.

GEORGE: Oh, Peter Mack. *(Recognizes the name)* How do you do?

PETER: How do you do?

GEORGE: And this is Michael Milick.

OTHERS: Hello. Hello.

MICHAEL: Hello.

JANE: American?

MICHAEL: Yes.

PETER: You can tell from one "hello"?

JANE: Can't you?

GEORGE: Michael's been here for years now, or so he's been telling me.

PETER: Then we won't have to worry about him starting to act American.

JANE: How long is "for years"?

MICHAEL: Nearly five now, I figure five more and you'll have me civilized.

(They laugh.)

OTHERS: Cheers.

MICHAEL: Sorry, I don't have a glass.

ANNIE: *(Coming up to* MICHAEL*)* Michael, did Carol find you? She was looking for you. Excuse me.

MICHAEL: This is George. This is—.

JANE: Jane.

MICHAEL: Jane. This is Peter Mack. My wife, Annie.

OTHERS: How do you do?

PETER: Have we met?

ANNIE: I work for Carol Howard.

PETER: Of course,

GEORGE: And married to an American? We let you girls do that, do we?

JANE: Are you an agent then too, Michael?

MICHAEL: No. Carol Howard's my agent. I translate.

PETER: Into American?

(Laughs)

ANNIE: No, from German.

MICHAEL: And now maybe from Polish. I'm about to start working on a novel by Janusz Vukosovic. Do you know him?

JANE: Janusz Vuk—

MICHAEL: Vukosovic.

JANE: Those Polish names.

PETER: Never heard of him.

(Music gets louder.)

MICHAEL: He's very well-known in Poland.

GEORGE: And as Poland goes— *(Laughs)*

MICHAEL: *(Trying to speak over the music)* Two or three of his books have done very well in French.

ANNIE: And also in Italian. Carol thinks—.

JANE: Who's the publisher?

MICHAEL: Here?

JANE: Yes, in London.

MICHAEL: There isn't one yet.

JANE: Ah. But there soon will be, won't there?

ANNIE: We're sure of it.

MICHAEL: Actually, Mr Mack, perhaps when I get a few chapters done, one of your editors could -

(Music loud:)

PETER: What? I can't...

MICHAEL: I think he's one of the most important Eastern European novelists today!

PETER: *(Having to almost shout now over the music)* Who?

MICHAEL: Vukosovic!!

ANNIE: He's sort of like a Polish Norman Mailer, Mr Mack!

(Short pause. Loud music)

MICHAEL: Or a Polish John LeCarre!!

(Cut out)

3.
A favor is done.

(Interior. MICHAEL and ANNIE's flat [Chiswick]. Bedroom and bathroom. Night)

(Footsteps. Light switched on in the bathroom. MICHAEL begins to brush his teeth.)

(Pause)

ANNIE: Well, how? is it?

MICHAEL: I thought you were asleep.

ANNIE: I was. How is it?

MICHAEL: I'm sorry if I woke—.

ANNIE: Michael, how's the bloody book? I've been sitting on pins.

MICHAEL: You were asleep sitting on...? *(Beat)* It's good, Annie. It is good. Thank God. *(Beat)* It is good. *(Beat)* Now I'll go back to sleep.

MICHAEL: I like it a whole lot. *(Beat)* It's pretty damn good.

(Short pause)

ANNIE: Pretty damn good?

(Short pause)

MICHAEL: I don't know. Maybe I shouldn't have read it at night.

ANNIE: Oh Christ, it's bad.

MICHAEL: It's not bad. *(Beat)* It is not bad. *(Pause)* It's about a guy who's lost most of his hair. And so he goes out and buys this hair piece which he only puts on when he goes to bed with his wife. *(Beat)* He goes to bed with a lot of other women. But he only wears the hair piece for his wife.

(Pause)

ANNIE: That's it? *(Beat)* It's bad. Shit.

MICHAEL: That's the basic thing, yeh. I mean he—the guy—goes through a lot, but that is what it keeps coming back to. Screwing his wife while wearing a hair piece. *(Beat)* To be honest I don't get it.

ANNIE: Must be some sort of metaphor.

MICHAEL: Yeh. *(Beat)* So? *(Pause)* It's short at least—not even two hundred pages.

ANNIE: I thought it was like two hundred and twenty something.

MICHAEL: It starts on page twelve. And each new chapter starts half-way down the page. *(Short pause)* I could do it in three weeks. *(Short pause)* The Polish isn't that difficult. That's what I was worried about, but it's not. Not much dialect at all.

ANNIE: Michael, if it's no good—.

MICHAEL: Annie, I liked him!

ANNIE: Then have him to dinner. Take him to a football match! Why translate his novel?!

(Pause)

MICHAEL: You should see inhere he lives.

ANNIE: You told me.

MICHAEL: I have heard of him, Annie. In Poland he is somebody. *(Beat)* His whole flat could fit in here in our bedroom. *(Beat)* If I turned him down...

ANNIE: What? What awful thing would happen?

MICHAEL: I don't know. *(Short pause)* I called Carol. Just before I finished tonight. I wanted to know more about him. *(Beat)* She said he's got a wife and three kids he's trying to get out.

ANNIE: And live on what?

MICHAEL: This book I suppose.

ANNIE: Oh God.

(Pause)

MICHAEL: Well, it is not all that terrible. There are some quite funny parts. *(Beat)* Some amusing bits. *(Short pause)* Who knows maybe there's a chance of actually getting it published. I can talk to John at Faber's. Maybe he can slip it by. *(Short pause)* Though I think we can forget Peter Mack.

ANNIE: Yes.

(Short pause)

MICHAEL: I mean, what is the worst that can happen? *(Beat)* I'll be practicing my Polish. *(Beat)* I'll be spending some time getting to know Janusz. I'm sure that'll be a hoot. *(Beat)* When you think what it means to… *(Short pause)* Hell, Annie, what's to lose?

(Fade out)

4.
Tea and biscuits given again.

(Interior. JANUSZ's *flat. Day)*

JANUSZ: *(Reads:)* "The Bald Spot by Janusz Vukosovic." *(Beat)* This is a good title?

MICHAEL: It's your title, Janusz. *(Beat)* Basically.

JANUSZ: Excuse me, I was getting you a plate for the biscuits…

MICHAEL: I'm really fine like— *(Short pause)* "(Polish word)" means "bald spot", Janusz. *(Beat)* Technically—literally—of course, it means what? "Hair piece." "Toupee." But— *(Short pause)* Believe me, The Bald Spot is a terrific title for the book. Sounds very… *(Beat)* It's very European. Eastern European. *(Beat)* Annie thinks so too.

JANUSZ: Annie?

MICHAEL: My wife.

JANUSZ: Of course. We haven't met.

MICHAEL: No. She loves the title. *(Beat)* She's English.

JANUSZ: Then she ought to know.

(Pause)

MICHAEL: Annie even said—

(Kettle boils.)

JANUSZ: I'm sorry.

(JANUSZ *goes to the kettle, it stops boiling.*)

MICHAEL: Annie said—. She was imagining, you know, an older British couple walking down the road, one turns to the other and says— "Oh Robert, look in the window of that bookshop. *The Hair Piece*, now there's a book I'd like to curl up with. *(He laughs.)* The Hair Piece. *(Laughs)* Ridiculous, isn't it, when it's translated. It sounds... *(Laughs)* You see what I mean. Why we needed to make it *The Bald Spot*.

(Pause)

JANUSZ: Here's your tea, Michael. *(Pause. Reads:)* "*The Bald Spot* by Janusz Vukosovic."

(JANUSZ *sits in a very creaky chair.*)

JANUSZ: This week I shall buy another chair that is not broken.

MICHAEL: Please, sit—.

JANUSZ: No, no.

(Pause. Chair creaks.)

MICHAEL: You don't have to read what I've done now. I could come back...

(Short pause)

JANUSZ: I am sorry, I read English very very slowly.

MICHAEL: That's okay. Look, I'll come back tomorrow. *(Beat)* You should take your time. *(Beat)* I'll keep working. I don't think I'm too far off with those first ten pages. *(Beat)* Style—that's what I'm most nervous about. *(Beat)* If I've gotten the style right. *(Beat)* Close enough. *(Pause)* I'll finish my tea and leave you alone then. *(Beat)* And come back. Tomorrow?

JANUSZ: *The Bald Spot.* Yes. *(Beat)* Our Minister of Defense wears a hair piece. *(Beat)* In Poland... In

Warsaw, you say "hair piece" and everyone thinks—
Minister of Defense. *(Beat)* I don't suppose you do here.

MICHAEL: What? Think "Polish Minister of Defense" when we hear "hair piece"?

JANUSZ: Yes.

MICHAEL: No. *(Laughs lightly to himself)* We don't think that. *(Beat)* I don't. *(Beat)* I can guarantee you that.

(Pause. JANUSZ *creaks in the chair.)*

MICHAEL: Janusz, you mean, it's a reference then? The title? *(Beat)* To the Polish Minister of Defense?

(Short pause)

JANUSZ: Please, eat a biscuit. I bought this whole new package just for you.

(Fade out.)

5.
Michael gives a dinner and chairs.

(Interior. MICHAEL *and* ANNIE's *flat. Evening)*

(Footsteps up the stairs)

MICHAEL: *(Calls back down into the cellar:)* I'll be right back down, Janusz! *(Beat. Quietly:)* What do you think—should we ask him to stay for dinner? *(Beat)* We can get Indian.

ANNIE: I might have a chicken.

JANUSZ: Whatever. I just think he'd like it. God knows how he feeds himself. He doesn't even have a kitchen.

ANNIE: I'll see what I need. *(Starts to walk away)* Michael?

MICHAEL: What?

ANNIE: I like him. I really do. *(Beat)* I see what you mean.

MICHAEL: He's a fascinating bugger, isn't he? I better go back down and see what he's found.

(As MICHAEL *goes back down the cellar steps:)*

MICHAEL: Find one you want, Janusz?

JANUSZ: *(In the cellar:)* I think it is between two.

MICHAEL: Then take them both if you want.

JANUSZ: No. No, I don't think I—

MICHAEL: Janusz, we have never even used either one of those chairs. They've been down here since Annie's mother died. *(Beat)* Take them. Please. *(Beat)* It's you who'll be doing us a favor. *(Short pause. He coughs.)* It's really dusty down here. *(Beat)* Come over here, I think there's a lamp you might like...

(Footsteps. Fade out. Cut to—the dining room, MICHAEL, ANNIE *and* JANUSZ *in the middle of dinner.)*

MICHAEL: More potatoes?

JANUSZ: Thank you. Yes. *(Beat)* So the last I hear is my wife and two of the children can leave, but the third child, she will have to stay with my mother-in-law.

ANNIE: They can do that?

JANUSZ: Of course, yes.

ANNIE: But that's like kidnapping, Michael.

JANUSZ: It is not that I do not like my mother-in-law...

ANNIE: No, no.

MICHAEL: That's not what Annie thought.

ANNIE: No.

JANUSZ: She still teaches in the school. Seventy-two years old. *(Beat)* Alzhbeta is ten.

MICHAEL: She's the one who would have to stay behind?

JANUSZ: Yes. She's the youngest.

(Pause. They eat.

ANNIE: Janusz, if there is anything that we—Michael and I—can— *(Beat)* Michael?

MICHAEL: I don't know what, Annie.

JANUSZ: Please. Please. *(Beat)* But I thank you. *(Short pause)* Anyway, my wife says she will wait until they can all leave together. This is what she says today. *(Beat)* In her last letter. *(Beat)* Either wait for this. Or I should come back.

MICHAEL: Is that a real possibility? Your going back?

(Pause)

JANUSZ: Delicious chicken, Annie.

ANNIE: Thank you.

(Short pause)

MICHAEL: I'll open another bottle of wine.

(Pause)

ANNIE: Michael? I was just thinking, you know Father's cottage in East Sussex? *(Beat)* No one ever goes there anymore.

MICHAEL: You mean for Janusz?

JANUSZ: No, no, please!

ANNIE: To use when you wanted. Mot to move there.

JANUSZ: Of course, I didn't think—

MICHAEL: It's in a beautiful spot.

ANNIE: Gorgeous! Incredibly quiet.

JANUSZ: Really, I don't—.

MICHAEL: After dinner we'll show you some photos—.

LANGUAGES SPOKEN HERE

ANNIE: The truth is, you'd be doing us the favor.

JANUSZ: Thank you. *(Beat)* Thanks.

(Pause. They eat.)

JANUSZ: So tell me, Michael, does one finally adjust to someone else's country after five years?

MICHAEL: You mean me?

ANNIE: I think Michael's adjusted remarkably well.

MICHAEL: You think so?

ANNIE: I do. I really do.

MICHAEL: It wasn't that hard. The people are nice. Different of course from Americans. But on the whole—.

ANNIE: He means that they aren't so—. What's the word? Open-hearted?

MICHAEL: On the surface only, Annie. Once you are here—

ANNIE: I don't know. Maybe it's not only on the surface. On second thought, maybe you just haven't lived here long enough. *(Beat)* I mean, something like this isn't very common here.

JANUSZ: Like this?

MICHAEL: She means inviting you here. Someone we don't know very well.

ANNIE: That is very American.

JANUSZ: I see.

MICHAEL: I wouldn't go quite that far, but I know what she means. But to answer your question, I think it took me about a year before I felt pretty comfortable. Like I belonged in London, you know. *(Beat)* Before that it was pretty hard. *(Short pause)* Especially when I'd find myself around, you know, what you'd call the very

Left-wing people. Those people would rather not even be seen with an American. It's stupid prejudice really, but—.

JANUSZ: And so it made you feel like there was something you had done.

MICHAEL: Yes. *(Beat)* That's right. *(Beat)* You must know the feeling. Anyway, for awhile I was very lonely.

JANUSZ: *(While eating:)* Then you didn't have—?

ANNIE: Me? I came later. You'd been here what? Two years? But don't let him kid you, Janusz, he wasn't as lonely as all that.

(ANNIE *laughs.* JANUSZ *laughs.*)

MICHAEL: Laugh if you want. Make fun of my suffering. More wine?

(MICHAEL *pours wine. Pause*)

MICHAEL: But I'm not saying there aren't things about the States that I miss. You've never been, right?

JANUSZ: No.

MICHAEL: Neither has Annie, but we're hoping to fix that, aren't we?

ANNIE: We'll see, Michael. *(Beat)* Let's see.

MICHAEL: Michigan is a very beautiful state. It's one of the states that has everything. Big cities. Big beaches. Farms. Lakes. The Upper Peninsula is—. Well, I'm not sure they even let cars in some places. It is that spectacular. *(Beat)* That's where Hemingway spent a lot of his time.

JANUSZ: I thought that was Cuba.

MICHAEL: There too. Also in Upper Michigan.

(Short pause)

JANUSZ: Is that where he killed himself?

MICHAEL: No, no, that's Idaho. *(Beat)* That's also very pretty.

(Beat. JANUSZ *Laughs to himself.)*

MICHAEL: What?

JANUSZ: Nothing.

(Short pause)

MICHAEL: *(While eating)* Annie and I have been thinking of spending a summer there. Right?

ANNIE: First we have to figure out how to afford it.

MICHAEL: Mostly it's the airfare. *(Short pause)* You know, Annie, we could camp out. They have a million camping grounds, Janusz.

JANUSZ: I see.

MICHAEL: *(To* ANNIE:*)* I had this idea that we buy a lot of the stuff over here, and then after we go camping we sell it back over there. *(Beat)* That's if we bought Norwegian or Swedish stuff. If we bought really good stuff that's really expensive in the States. *(Short pause)* My parents would love it if we came. *(Beat)* They came over here about two years ago. Two years ago?

ANNIE: Yeh. *(Beat)* I liked them both. Very nice people.

(Short pause)

MICHAEL: They had the time of their lives, let me tell you. *(Beat)* They fell for Annie in a second. And she was nervous as anything.

ANNIE: Who was nervous?

MICHAEL: What about at the airport—

ANNIE: Okay. Okay.

(Sound begins to fade out.)

MICHAEL: Janusz—

JANUSZ: Yes?

MICHAEL: While we were waiting for my parents to clear customs, it was like Annie's jaw was frozen solid.

ANNIE: Janusz—

JANUSZ: Yes?

ANNIE: That was not nerves. That was a typically English expression.

(ANNIE *and* MICHAEL *laugh.*)

MICHAEL: They loved London, didn't they?

ANNIE: Janusz—

JANUSZ: Yes?

ANNIE: They loved everything about it.

MICHAEL: We started off with Buckingham Palace of course.

ANNIE: Janusz-

JANUSZ: Yes?

ANNIE: You're not going to believe this—.

MICHAEL: Let me tell him. Annie had never even seen the changing of the—.

(Sound out)

6.
Janusz thanks Michael.

(Interior. JANUSZ's *flat. Day)*

(JANUSZ *clears his throat.)*

(Short pause)

(JANUSZ *goes to the sink, turns on the tap and fills the kettle with water.)*

(Pause)

LANGUAGES SPOKEN HERE

JANUSZ: Michael? *(Beat)* Have you finished reading? *(Beat)* Is something the matter? *(Short pause)* It stopped raining outside. Perhaps you'd like to get some air. *(Beat)* You see how little I changed what you'd done, Michael. One word. *(Beat)* Maybe two words. *(Beat)* For the style only.

(Pause)

MICHAEL: It's totally different.

(Pause)

JANUSZ: A few words. I very much liked some of what you had done.

MICHAEL: Janusz, you changed everything. There's hardly a line of mine left in the ten pages.

JANUSZ: The first pages are always the most difficult. It is with them that one learns the feeling. You are learning now the feeling, Michael.

MICHAEL: Yeh. *(Beat)* I guess.

JANUSZ: And you shall get that feeling in no time at all. *(Beat)* It's all that German you've been translating, This is what confuses one. *(Laughs)* Still some of your word choices—excellent. *(Beat)* Excellent. *(Short pause)* What do you say, today I shall join you in a cup of tea.

(JANUSZ *goes to the sink, he washes a cup.*)

MICHAEL: By the way, you spelled a couple of words wrong.

JANUSZ: Spelling in English! This is my nightmare! Thank you for pointing this out.

(Short pause)

MICHAEL: Least there's something I can do.

JANUSZ: Michael. *(Beat)* The chairs fit nicely into here, yes? *(Beat)* And the lamp too. Thank you. I can't thank you and Annie enough. What a lucky man you are,

Michael, with such a cook for a wife! *(Short pause)*
And this Michigan. What a place it must be. I can only
imagine it like a dream. But perhaps I shall get the
chance to visit it myself one day. *(Beat)* Perhaps. *(Short
pause)* To bring me into your home like that. I am very
grateful...

MICHAEL: Janusz, you don't have to try to make me feel
better... *(Beat)* I just had a different take on the book,
that's all. *(Beat)* Now that I see what you want—.

JANUSZ: Of course.

(Pause)

MICHAEL: I missed—. I didn't realize you meant it to be
so—ironic, I guess.

JANUSZ: Ironic! This is Polish literature! *(Laughs.
Pause)* Let me tell you a story, Michael. About Polish
Literature.

MICHAEL: Janusz—

JANUSZ: Please. I think this will help us to understand
each other.

MICHAEL: I know what you're going to—.

JANUSZ: Michael. *(Short pause)* This was what? Maybe
three years ago. In Warsaw of course. At our Writers'
Union offices, there was a party. *(Beat)* A meeting. A
small meeting with music, wine and vodka. *(Beat)* A
party. *(He laughs to himself.)* Very small. Maybe twelve,
fifteen of us all talking, meeting, putting, as one says,
names to faces. I was in one corner talking to a very
attractive poetess. *(Beat)* I have since read her poetry
and her most distinguished attribute remains her
attractiveness.

(Kettle boils.)

JANUSZ: One moment. *(Takes kettle off)* She knew my
books of course.

LANGUAGES SPOKEN HERE 27

MICHAEL: Of course.

(*As* JANUSZ *continues to pours the hot water for the tea:*)

JANUSZ: Occasionally at these "meetings" someone will read a work—always a short work, this we make the rule; the shorter the better. *(Beat)* It is maybe five o'clock in the afternoon, no one has begun to read yet, though my poetess has moved very close to me; she has her shoes off and leans against the grey wall, her arm out; and if I were to lean back as well, this arm would be around me or at least against my shoulders. *(Beat)* She has lovely feet I see. She wears nylons. *(Beat)* And her breath is quite warm as she asks about the women in my books. What women are you most interested in, I ask. *(Beat)* The matrons or the—. But I never got the question out, Michael, because just then the door to the hall opens and two policemen and a man who we soon hear is Russian hurry in. Someone asks what they are doing as this is a private meeting. *(Beat)* The Russian—who is drunk by the way—he turns to a small woman—the name doesn't matter, and with the back of his hand hits her in the face. She screams. Her nose starts to bleed. She is one of our best literary critics, this woman, an expert on Conrad. At least fifty years old as well. *(Beat)* The Russian tells her to sit on the floor. He then lifts up her dress, and with a violent gesture he rips off her pants. Her underpants. *(Short pause)* I forgot to buy biscuits. I'm sorry.

MICHAEL: That's okay.

JANUSZ: One of our best playwrights—a surrealist—tries to stop this but is knocked unconscious before he can get to her. Standing next to the attractive poetess, I wonder if he is going to make us all strip, when suddenly he comes right up to me and says—"Janusz Vukosovic?" *(Beat)* I nod. *(Beat)* "The novelist Vukosovic?" He'd recognized my face from a picture on one of my novels. Two have been published in Russian. *(Beat)* Very popular. *(Beat)* He speaks to me in Russian. He says what is he to do? He's got this old critic naked on the floor, but already he's lost his taste for her. He wonders if I would trade him my poetess for the critic. *(Beat)* I say I cannot make such decisions. *(Beat)* He says then he shall take them both. So I decide quickly. The critic is very important, this I know. And the poetess—I did not know her work. Fortunately, it turned out not to be so good as I have said, but then I did not know this. Still I took the chance. And make the trade. And with the help of the policemen, she is taken out of the room. *(Beat)* You see the responsibilities thrust upon the writer in my country?

(Pause)

MICHAEL: Yes. *(Short pause)* Janusz—

JANUSZ: One moment. Now I tell you this story to make a point.

MICHAEL: Janusz, I understand the point. Because someone like me hasn't experienced this what? Hell? Suffering? Degradation? Then I can't, I don't—. It is maybe impossible for me to really translate—.

JANUSZ: Michael. *(Beat)* Oh Michael. *(He laughs.)*

MICHAEL: What?

JANUSZ: That is not my point. *(Beat)* My point is—that you believe the story, yes?

MICHAEL: I—

JANUSZ: This story I just make up right now, you believed it. Not even a good story. *(Beat)* Russians stay a million miles away from people like me in Poland. *(Beat)* But you believe. And Michael this is your first nature, to believe what you hear, what you are told. *(Short pause)* To translate Polish one must relearn one's first nature, Michael. *(Beat)* One must learn to think like

I do. *(Beat)* One must learn that what is in front of one, what one sees and hears with one's own eyes and ears is usually what is not true. *(Beat)* And certainly not to be believed. *(Beat)* More tea?

(Fade out)

7.
Janusz gives a dinner and a shawl.

(Interior. [Later exterior]. JANUSZ's *flat. Evening)*

*(*MICHAEL, ANNIE, JANUSZ *and* JAN KOSTKA *having dinner.)*

MICHAEL: Delicious curry.

ANNIE: Yes. You must have quite a good Indian place in the area.

JANUSZ: Yes. Yes, there is. *(Beat)* Very nice.

(Short pause)

JAN: *(In Czech:)* What did they say?

JANUSZ: *(In Czech:)* They like the food.

JAN: *(In Czech:)* It's from the corner?

JANUSZ: *(In Czech:)* The place on Edgeware Road is much cheaper.

(Pause. They eat.)

MICHAEL: Yes. Very nice.

JAN: *(In Czech:)* What?

JANUSZ: *(To* JAN, *in Czech:)* Why don't you try to speak Polish? He understands Polish. *(To* MICHAEL, *in English:)* I am trying to convince Jan to try to speak Polish.

MICHAEL: Oh. He speaks—

JANUSZ: Not too good. But...

MICHAEL: I'm sorry I don't speak Czech.

ANNIE: Does he know any German. Michael's fluent in German, and I can sort of follow along...

JANUSZ: No. *(Beat)* He doesn't speak German. *(Beat. In Czech:)* You don't speak German do you?

JAN: *(In Czech:)* No.

JANUSZ: He said—.

MICHAEL: Yes. We figured that out.

(Short pause. They eat.)

MICHAEL: How long has Jan been here, Janusz?

JANUSZ: He arrived only before you and Annie did.

MICHAEL: No. I meant—

JANUSZ: Oh, in England you mean. Four months. *(Beat)* That was stupid of me when you asked—.

MICHAEL: Not at all. I wasn't being clear.

(Short pause)

JANUSZ: Four months he's been here. *(In Czech:)* You've been here four months, right?

JAN: *(In Czech:)* It's been more than four months, Janusz. It is May, yes? 1 came in December. So that's December, January February, March, April, and May. That's six months. *(Beat)* Almost six months.

JANUSZ: *(In Czech:)* You came on December 30th. And It's only May what? Third. No, fourth. That's not six month.

JAN: *(In Czech:)* Five months then.

JANUSZ: *(In Czech:)* That's not even five months. It's what I told them—four months. *(Beat)* Four months and a few days. *(Beat. In English:)* Don't pay any attention to him. He's been here four months.

MICHAEL: Ah.

(Pause. They eat.)

JANUSZ: Michael, perhaps you could tell Jan where the Czechs are in America.

MICHAEL: Where the Czechs are? *(Beat)* I'm sorry, I don't understand.

JANUSZ: Like the Poles are in this Michigan. Where are the Czechs?

(Short pause)

MICHAEL: Probably all around the country. *(Beat)* I don't know to be honest.

JANUSZ: *(In Czech:)* He doesn't know where the Czechs are in America.

JAN: *(In Czech:)* There are no Czechs in America.

JANUSZ: That can't be true. *(In English:)* Jan says there are no Czechs in America.

MICHAEL: I doubt if that's—

JAN: *(In Czech:)* Once you go to America you become American.

JANUSZ: Ah. *(Beat)* He says you go to America you become American. Not Czech anymore.

MICHAEL: Oh. *(Laughs)* Yes. I guess in a way that's true. That's sort of what worries Annie actually.

ANNIE: What worries me?

MICHAEL: I think that's why you're a little hesitant about going to the States. Even for a short visit. *(Beat)* Let alone moving there.

JANUSZ: You're thinking of moving—?

ANNIE: No. *(Beat)* No, we're not, Janusz.

(Short pause)

MICHAEL: She's afraid, Janusz of losing something of herself.

ANNIE: I never said that, Michael.

MICHAEL: Not in those words—.

ANNIE: Then that means I never said it. *(Beat)* What would I do in the States?

MICHAEL: That's why I've been suggesting we just go for a short—.

JANUSZ: One moment, please. Stop, please. Let me translate. *(In Czech:)* They're talking about moving or just yisiting the States. Michael says she is afraid of losing something of herself. She says she doesn't know what she will do there.

JAN: *(In Czech:)* I understand.

JANUSZ: You can continue now.

(Short pause)

ANNIE: I'm not worried about visiting your parents in the States.

MICHAEL: I know you're not. *(Beat)* Janusz, could I get some more wine?

JANUSZ: Of course. Here, let me. I'm sorry.

(Pause)

ANNIE: Janusz, have you thought any more about my father's cottage]

JAN: *(In Czech:)* What's this?

JANUSZ: *(In Czech:)* They have offered me the use of a cottage in the country.

JAN: *(In Czech:)* Where is it?

JANUSZ: Where was it again?

ANNIE: East Sussex. *(Beat)* Not terribly far really.

JAN: East Sussex?

ANNIE: Yes.

JAN: *(In Czech:)* Are you going to use it?

JANUSZ: *(In Czech:)* I doubt it. Why would I want to go to the—

JAN: *(In Czech:)* Then I'll use it.

JANUSZ: *(In Czech:)* Jan, they asked me.

JAN: *(In Czech:)* If it's Just sitting there…

JANUSZ: Excuse us. *(In Czech:)* I can't just—

JAN: *(In Czech:)* Why not, if they're offering. Ask them. *(Beat)* Ask them.

(Short pause)

JANUSZ: Jan says if I don't use the cottage he would like to. *(Beat)* But I told him—.

ANNIE: No. No. *(Beat)* I'll have to ask my father, of course. But I'm sure, he'll—. *(Beat)* Make sure we get his number before we go.

JAN: *(In Czech:)* Tell them I used to have a cottage about fifty-five kilometers outside of Prague.

JANUSZ: Jan says he used to have a cottage outside of Prague.

JAN: *(In Czech:)* And if they are ever in Prague, I know the woman who has it now.

JANUSZ: And if you are ever in Prague, the woman who has the cottage now, he knows.

MICHAEL: Oh. *(Beat)* Thank you,

ANNIE: Thank you, Jan.

(Pause. JANUSZ *gets up out of his seat.)*

JANUSZ: Excuse me.

(JANUSZ *walks to a closet, opens the door, takes something out and walks back to the table.)*

JANUSZ: Here.

ANNIE: What's...?

JANUSZ: It is for you. Actually it is to thank both of you. But I thought—. *(Beat)* Open it.

MICHAEL: Open it, Annie.

ANNIE: Janusz, I hope you didn't spend your money on—.

(ANNIE *has opened the package.*)

ANNIE: It's beautiful. Look Michael.

MICHAEL: What is it?

ANNIE: A shawl?

JANUSZ: Yes. *(Beat)* I found it in a stall at Covent Garden. *(Beat)* I think it's Polish.

JAN: *(In Czech:)* Let me see.

JANUSZ: He wants to see. *(Beat)* It's for the chairs. And the lamp. *(In Czech:)* They loaned me these chairs.

JAN: *(In Czech:)* Nice chairs. Have they any more to loan?

JANUSZ: *(In Czech:)* Jan, I can't ask

JAN: *(In Czech:)* Ask. Why not?

ANNIE: What? Does Jan want something?

JANUSZ: He wants to know if you have any more chairs.

MICHAEL: Any more chairs?

JANUSZ: I told him you loaned—

MICHAEL: Oh. *(Beat)* Well, I'm sure we probably do. We must make sure to get Jan's number, Annie.

JANUSZ: *(In Czech:)* They have more chairs.

JAN: *(In Czech:)* I told you, Janusz.

(Pause)

ANNIE: The shawl's hand embroidered, isn't it?

JANUSZ: Yes.

(Short pause)

ANNIE: Janusz, you really shouldn't be spending your money on us. *(Beat)* On me.

JANUSZ: It is the least I can do to pay you both back.

MICHAEL: Janusz, but we've told you, taking those chairs was actually doing us a—.

JAN: *(In Czech:)* You gave the shawl to her?

JANUSZ: *(In Czech:)* Yes.

JAN: *(In Czech:)* And not to your wife, Marie? She would love such a shawl.

JANUSZ: *(In Czech, shouts:)* I didn't buy it for Marie!

MICHAEL: What? What did he say?

JAN: *(In Czech:)* She's there with your children—

JANUSZ: *(In Czech:)* I gave it to—

ANNIE: Who's Marie?

JANUSZ: My wife.

MICHAEL: He knows your wife?

JANUSZ: We've known each other for many years. He's a good friend of my wife's.

JAN: *(In Czech:)* A shawl like this would have made her so happy.

MICHAEL: What's he saying?

JANUSZ: Nothing.

JAN: *(In Czech:)* Right now, she is wondering if you even remember her.

JANUSZ: He says I should have given the shawl to my wife.

ANNIE: Yes. Of course he's right. Here.

JANUSZ: But I didn't buy it for my wife. I bought it for you, who have been so kind to me.

ANNIE: Really, it would make me feel—

JANUSZ: *(Yells:)* No!!!

(Pause)

JAN: *(In Czech:)* You ought to be ashamed of yourself.

ANNIE: What did he say?

JANUSZ: That I should be ashamed.

JAN: *(In Czech:)* And it would serve you right if Marie were in bed with someone right this minute.

JANUSZ: And that it would serve me right if my wife were in bed with someone this very minute.

(Pause. Akward silence.

MICHAEL: More wine anyone?

ANNIE: I would, please, Michael.

MICHAEL: Janusz?

JANUSZ: No.

(Short pause)

MICHAEL: Jan?

JAN: *(In Czech:)* I never say no to French wine.

JANUSZ: He says he can't say no to French wine.

MICHAEL: It's Italian wine.

JAN: *(In Czech:)* Or Italian wine.

JANUSZ: Or Italian wine.

(Fade out and cut to:)

(Exterior. The street. Night)

(MICHAEL *and* ANNIE *walking to the tube.*)

(Pause)

ANNIE: That was nice. *(Short pause)* That was interesting.

MICHAEL: Are you really going to talk to your father—?

ANNIE: About Jan using the cottage? Of course not. You saw how much he smoked. *(Beat)* Even during dinner. *(Beat)* I didn't know people did that anymore. While other people are eating. *(Beat)* I'm afraid he'd burn the cottage down.

(Short pause)

MICHAEL: I forgot to get his number.

ANNIE: Oh well.

(Pause as ANNIE and MICHAEL walk)

MICHAEL: Beautiful shawl.

ANNIE: I wish he hadn't spent—. And Jan was right he should have sent it to his wife. Think of what it must be like for her.

MICHAEL: But I guess he felt he owed us so much...

ANNIE: That's silly.

MICHAEL: I know that. *(Beat)* You know that. *(Beat)* But— *(Short pause)* It was obviously just very important for him not to feel too—. I don't know, in debt, I guess, to someone else. *(Beat)* For his own self-respect, I mean. *(Beat)* So this was his way of paying us back.

ANNIE: The curry was awful.

MICHAEL: Wasn't it.

(Beat)

ANNIE: So anyway, in his mind, we're all even now.

MICHAEL: Yes. *(Beat)* Now we're even.

(Fade out)

8.
Michael thanks Janusz.

(Interior. JANUSZ's *flat. Day)*

(Door buzzer)

(Pause)

(Buzzer)

(Short pause)

(Buzzer)

(Footsteps. JANUSZ *opens the door.)*

JANUSZ: Sorry, I'm just on the telephone.

(As JANUSZ *and* MICHAEL *walk back in:)*

JANUSZ: Michael, you know where the kettle is.

MICHAEL: Don't worry about me. Take your time.

(Short pause)

JANUSZ: *(Into the phone:)* Hello, yes. That sounds good, yes. *(Beat)* No, I don't. But I take your word for it. *(Beat)* Uh-huh. But could we talk about this later, Michael Milick has just come in. *(Beat)* Yes. Thank you. Goodbye. *(Hangs up. Short pause)* You didn't put the kettle on.

*(*JANUSZ *turns on the tap and fills the kettle. Pause)*

JANUSZ: Sit down, please Michael. *(Beat)* I apologize, I haven't had time to get your biscuits for this morning. *(Beat)* But I could go right—.

MICHAEL: Janusz, I don't need any biscuits.

JANUSZ: No?

MICHAEL: No. Really. *(Beat)* Who was on the phone?

JANUSZ: You mean now? Come on, sit down, you shouldn't wait to be asked, Michael. *(Short pause)* I hope my friend, Jan, didn't—how do you say it? Put you off last night.

MICHAEL: Not at all. Annie and I adored him.

JANUSZ: Good. He liked both of you very much.

MICHAEL: I'm glad.

JANUSZ: He's a very witty man—in Czech.

MICHAEL: I gathered this. *(Short pause)* It was a wonderful evening. Very special for both of us. We both wanted to thank you for inviting us.

JANUSZ: The pleasure was mine. *(Beat)* Let me get your cup. Today I think I shall join with you and have some tea.

(JANUSZ *goes to sink and washes cups.*)

MICHAEL: I'm sorry if I'm a little early, Janusz.

JANUSZ: You're early? *(Beat)* I did not realize.

(Short pause)

MICHAEL: There's nothing the matter, is there, Janusz?

JANUSZ: No, what could be the matter?

(Pause)

MICHAEL: Have you had the chance to go over the last twenty pages I gave you?

JANUSZ: Yes, yes, of course. Here. Look here. Hardly a single change or suggestion.

MICHAEL: *(After a short pause)* I'm amazed. *(Beat)* Grateful, but still amazed.

JANUSZ: It's the feeling. I told you once one gets the feeling then—

MICHAEL: Then I've finally gotten what you want. *(Beat)* This is what you want. *(Beat)* You are happy with this. Is that right? I don't want you to—. Just because—

JANUSZ: Just because what?

MICHAEL: Because we're—well friends.

JANUSZ: No, no, I wouldn't do that.

MICHAEL: Good. *(Short pause)* I have to admit I've started feeling a lot better about my work. I do think I've started to hear your voice—.

JANUSZ: Yes, yes.

(Short pause)

MICHAEL: Well, let's hope it's not a fluke and the next ten pages are as good.

JANUSZ: I'm sure—.

MICHAEL: Well, let's see, right? *(Beat)* Just keep being tough on me, okay?

JANUSZ: Okay.

(Short pause)

MICHAEL: Nothing's wrong? You haven't heard something about your wife and children?

JANUSZ: No, no. *(Beat)* What could be wrong?

MICHAEL: I don't know, you seem-

JANUSZ: That's the wine from last night, not wanting to leave my head.

(JANUSZ *laughs.* MICHAEL *laughs.*)

MICHAEL: Yes, that could be it.

(Short pause)

JANUSZ: *(Suddenly energetic:)* Oh, you asked who was on the phone.

MICHAEL: Only because I heard you mention my name—as if they knew me.

JANUSZ: Yes, of course he knows you. You introduced us, in a way. *(Beat)* John Robertson at Fabers.

MICHAEL: John? I didn't know you two—

(Kettle boils.)

JANUSZ: Excuse me.

(Kettle stops boiling.)

JANUSZ: Didn't I tell you? We had lunch together just the other day. *(Beat)* I thought I told you, Michael.

MICHAEL: No, you didn't. *(Beat)* What did he want? Did you give him some chapters?

JANUSZ: Yes and he's reading them. That's what he called to say.

MICHAEL: He called to say he was reading them?

JANUSZ: Yes.

MICHAEL: Just to say that?

JANUSZ: Yes.

MICHAEL: Not that he liked what he'd read, only that he was still—

JANUSZ: Yes. *(Beat)* Here's your tea. *(Pause)* He took me to a restaurant in Chelsea. *(Beat)* We ate Italian. *(Pause)* Faber and Faber, this is T S Eliot's publisher, yes?

MICHAEL: It was. It is. *(Beat)* He worked there too. And they published his books.

(Short pause)

JANUSZ: Eliot is a very good poet, Michael. One of your best. I like Eliot.

MICHAEL: Good.

(Short pause)

JANUSZ: And Ezra Pound, no?

MICHAEL: They also publish Pound.

JANUSZ: Very over-rated poet, I think. In Polish his poems read like drivel.

MICHAEL: Maybe it's the translations.

JANUSZ: Yes? I guess that could be. *(Short pause)* But Eliot—. Very important. *(Beat)* This would be a good place for my book?

MICHAEL: Yes. Definitely. *(Beat)* If they show any interest at all, we should kill to get it published there.

JANUSZ: Yes.

(Fade out)

9.
Janusz plays his cards.

(Interior. MICHAEL *and* ANNIE's *flat [*MICHAEL's *study])*

(Afternoon)

*(*MICHAEL *typing.)*

(Pause)

(Knock on the door)

(After a moment the door opens, MICHAEL *continues to type.)*

MICHAEL: What are you doing home? *(Beat)* Just a second. *(He types. Then stops)* What time is it?

ANNIE: Half past two. *(Beat)* Carol thought I should come home.

MICHAEL: Is anything wrong? Are you sick?

ANNIE: No. *(Beat)* No, I'm not sick. *(Beat)* Carol thought it'd be best if I were the one to tell you. *(Beat)* She said she'd do it of course, but—.

MICHAEL: You were the one to tell me what, Annie?

ANNIE: Carol's really upset. You know, you are more than just a client to her.

MICHAEL: Annie! Please what are you talking about?

ANNIE: Actually it's unbelievable. I don't understand really. *(Beat)* John Robertson—

MICHAEL: Of Fabers. Yes.

ANNIE: He called Carol today. He said he suddenly remembered a conversation he'd had with you about— oh six weeks ago.

MICHAEL: I called him about Janusz's book. And Janusz told me this morning—.

ANNIE: Wait. *(Beat)* He said, well, he wanted you— through Carol of course—to know that Mr Vukosovic had been to see him.

MICHAEL: I know this. They had lunch.

ANNIE: Been to see him with someone else's translation of his book.

(Short pause)

MICHAEL: Say that again.

ANNIE: It seems Janusz has been working with someone else on translating his book, Michael. *(Beat)* They've been working for over a month now.

MICHAEL: Annie, I can't believe—.

ANNIE: It's true. Carol called Janusz and he confessed it. *(Short pause)* Hey, he's a son of a bitch, what can you do? *(Short pause)* He gets you to do the legwork, you make the connections—. Carol's never going to deal with Janusz again, I can tell you that. *(Beat)* Michael, I'm sorry.

MICHAEL: Who's the other translator?

ANNIE: Some Polish friend of his, I think.

MICHAEL: For Christ sake, why didn't he just—. I would have just stopped. *(Beat)* And Fabers?

ANNIE: They like the book. *(Beat)* Though Carol thinks if we kicked up a fuss, they'd shelve it.

MICHAEL: Shelve it?

ANNIE: It's already been bought. *(Beat)* The other translator has already been paid an advance. *(Beat)* And this you won't believe. Robertson says Janusz wants to use a few things from your work, sort of incorporate them in the other translation. *(Beat)* We think that Janusz would have been only too happy to take what he wanted without even asking. But Robertson is putting a stop to that. *(Beat)* This isn't Poland after all. *(Beat)* They'll need your permission. *(Pause)*

MICHAEL: Hell. *(Laughs to himself)* Look what I've been writing: a letter to *The Times*. I was going to send it around and get some big signatures on it, I'd hoped. *(Beat)* It's a plea for the release of Janusz's wife and all three kids.

(Short pause)

ANNIE: Fuck that now. *(Short pause)* I don't understand, he said nothing last night at dinner.

MICHAEL: Or this morning. *(Beat)* I saw him just this morning.

ANNIE: I'll get Carol, she wanted to speak to you as soon as—. *(She dials the phone.)*

MICHAEL: *(Into phone:)* Hello, Carol? Michael. *(Beat)* Yes. It breaks my heart too.

(Fade out)

10.
Janusz is granted another favor.

(Interior. JANUSZ's flat. Afternoon)

(Door buzzer. JANUSZ's footsteps as he goes to the door. He opens the door.)

JANUSZ: Annie, what a nice surprise. *(Beat)* Come in, come in.

(ANNIE *and* JANUSZ *come into the flat.*)

JANUSZ: Sit down.

ANNIE: I brought Michael's signed permission. *(Beat)* So you can use his—.

JANUSZ: Thank you. *(Beat)* But you needn't have come. The post would have been soon enough. *(Beat)* But I appreciate this. It must not have been an easy thing to give. This permission,

ANNIE: Janusz...

MICHAEL: Say what you want to say, Annie.

ANNIE: Janusz, people don't behave the way you did in civilized countries.

JANUSZ: Poland is civilized too. For many years now. *(Beat)* Keep Poland out of this, yes? *(Short pause)* Is he outside?

ANNIE: No.

JANUSZ: I would have thanked him in person. *(Short pause)* Annie, let me be very blunt.

ANNIE: Please. Be blunt. Or at the very least be honest for a change.

JANUSZ: Michael's work was not very good. His Polish is not...

ANNIE: So then why didn't you just tell him? Instead you work with him for a month.

JANUSZ: I wanted to. I tried to. *(Beat)* I thought maybe I could help him. *(Beat)* And I did for sometime. But...

(Short pause)

ANNIE: He went out and found you a publisher.

JANUSZ: He helped in this, yes. *(Beat)* And so my actions do not look so good, I admit. *(Beat)* But it is not like the book was never heard of.

ANNIE: Actually it is exactly like that.

JANUSZ: In Warsaw it is very successful. *(Short pause)* I am very grateful for what Michael did. Please, sit down. They are your chairs.

MICHAEL: He considered you a friend.

JANUSZ: I am his—.

ANNIE: And then you made him feel like a fool!

JANUSZ: Michael is no fool. I am sure translating German, he is much more—.

ANNIE: I didn't mean as a translator, Janusz. *(Beat)* Jesus Christ, he was doing you a favor and you turn around and—

JANUSZ: I am very sorry how it must look. After all I have to live here, yes? I don't want to be thought of in a bad way. *(Beat)* But to answer you, first I did not consider that he was doing me a favor.

ANNIE: He didn't even like the damn book.

JANUSZ: No. *(Beat)* No, that is not true.

ANNIE: He thought it was stupid.

JANUSZ: No. *(Beat)* Maybe. *(Beat)* Annie, I always made it very clear that I was first interested in making the book as good as it could be in English. I never hid this. And this is all I was doing.

ANNIE: To make it as successful as it could be you mean.

JANUSZ: Whatever. Whatever the criteria are. I do not know yet.

ANNIE: And this permits you to take advantage—.

JANUSZ: Perhaps! *(Beat)* All I do know is that being nice and doing favors has nothing to do with writing books or making art. *(Beat)* Being nice and doing favors is what one does between writing books and making art. While one is waiting to write the book or while resting from making the art. Friends are needed then. *(Short pause)* And Michael has been a very good friend. And I think I have been a very good friend to Michael.

ANNIE: Right. *(Laughs to herself)*

JANUSZ: *(Almost yelling now:)* Annie, if it was friendships I was most after—MY FRIENDS ARE IN WARSAW!! *(Beat)* If I did not write books, I could have stayed with my friends in Warsaw. *(Beat)* Is not this obvious about me?! *(Beat)* I can think of nothing more obvious about me than this. *(Short pause)* You think I came to England to be your friend? *(Beat)* This is not to say I do not wish to be your friend, Annie, or that I shall not try to be a good friend to you. But for God's sake, please be fair to me!!! *(Pause)* I am sorry if Michael is hurt. He will get over it very soon. *(Beat)* A bad translation, my book will never get over.

ANNIE: Okay. *(Beat)* I guess we pushed ourselves too much on you.

JANUSZ: That is not what I am saying!

(Short pause)

ANNIE: I was brought up to take my time getting to know someone, just to prevent this sort of—.

JANUSZ: Annie, damn it, you are not listening to me!!

ANNIE: We had you over to dinner.

JANUSZ: I had you too. *(Short pause)* Let me put the tea on.

ANNIE: We gave you chairs.

JANUSZ: Loaned them to me. *(Beat)* I gave you that shawl.

ANNIE: Which I brought back. I don't want it anymore.

JANUSZ: Annie, no. *(Beat)* No.

ANNIE: Give it to your wife.

JANUSZ: No.

(Pause)

ANNIE: We went so far out of our way to help you,

JANUSZ: I know. *(Beat)* Thank you.

(Pause as JANUSZ *turns the tap on and fills the kettle.)*

ANNIE: *(Finally:)* Is this how you treated your friends back in Warsaw?!

JANUSZ: Annie, I did much worse to them. *(Beat)* I came here.

(Fade out)

11.
Michael plays his cards.

(Interior. Restaurant [Chelsea]. Lunchtime)

WAITER: More coffee?

ANDREW: None for me. Two cups is my limit.

MICHAEL: No, thank you.

(Short pause)

ANDREW: Michael, would you like a taste of my pie?

MICHAEL: No thanks.

ANDREW: I've never eaten here.

MICHAEL: It's only something like three months old.

(Short pause)

ANDREW: So anyway, you in the end gave Vukosovic your permission.

MICHAEL: Yes. What could I do? *(Beat)* How would it have looked? *(Beat)* He has no money. He hardly knows anyone.

ANDREW: He knew another translator.

MICHAEL: I'm not bitter, Andrew.

ANDREW: I can't say I'd blame you if you were. If I were in your shoes—

MICHAEL: You'd be acting the same way. *(Beat)* Once I got over the initial shock—the sense of betrayal—I soon realized there was little I could do.

(Short pause)

ANDREW: Anyone going to review this book?

MICHAEL: I had lunch last week with Lester—.

ANDREW: He's still at the *Review of Books*?

MICHAEL: Yes. *(Beat)* He isn't going to touch it. No review. Nothing. *(Beat)* That's a shame, I think. *(Beat)* It's not a bad book, really. A little obscure for a British—and certainly for an American—audience. But—. Worthy of some sort of review.

ANDREW: *(Eating his pie)* Well—serves him right, if you ask me. This sort of behavior, I'd hate to see it encouraged. What about the dailies?

MICHAEL: Lester doubted if there'd be anything. *(Beat)* He was going to talk to some people. *(Beat)* He was very put off by the way I was treated. I couldn't convince him that I didn't care—.

ANDREW: Lester would be put off. He's a man of high moral standards.

MICHAEL: As you are, Andrew.

ANDREW: I like to think so, yes.

(Pause)

MICHAEL: In the end, what I feel most for Janusz is pity. And to think he brought it all on himself. *(Beat)* Really, didn't he know that no one would want to work with someone who acted like—.

ANDREW: Yes, it's not like he were bloody Samuel Beckett or something, then—well. But he's not, of course. *(Beat)* This play he gave me, well, it's okay. It's just okay.

MICHAEL: I felt the sane way when I read it in Polish.

ANDREW: I have to confess I was leaning a little toward doing it. It is after all—okay. *(Beat)* And how many plays are okay today? *(Laughs to himself)*

MICHAEL: Janusz will be terribly excited to hear this.

ANDREW: But to be honest I'm beginning to change my mind.

MICHAEL: I hope not because of—

ANDREW: You do a man's play, well, you spend a lot of time with the man. And life is only so long, Michael. *(Beat)* I may just send the script right back.

MICHAEL: But if it's worth doing—.

ANDREW: It's only okay, Michael. Nothing more.

(Pause)

MICHAEL: He really has fucked things up for himself, hasn't he?

ANDREW: Indeed so, Michael. Indeed.

WAITER: Anything else, gentlemen?

MICHAEL: Just the check. *(Beat)* Andrew, please, this is on me. I really do insist.

ANDREW: Then, thank you, Michael. Thank you very much.

MICHAEL: You're welcome.

(Fade out)

END OF PLAY

EATING WORDS

EATING WORDS was first broadcast as part of the Globe Theatre Season, on B B C Radio 4/World Service on October 30, 1989. The cast was as follows;

HENRY	John Woodvine
VANESSA	Sheila Allen
SAM	Ed Asner
YOUNG WOMAN IN PUB	Emily Richard
WAITER	Charles Simpson
People in restaurant & pub	Vincent Brimble, John Bull, David King, Elizabeth Mansfield, Simon Treves, Joe Dunlop, Christopher Good, Danny Schiller
Director	Ned Chaillet

CHARACTERS & SETTING

HENRY, *an English writer in his fifties.*
VANESSA, *his older sister.*
SAM, *an American writer in his early fifties*
YOUNG WOMAN IN THE PUB
WAITER

The play takes place in London.
The time is the present.

for Ned Chaillet

1.
Henry and Sam get together twice-a-year for lunch.

(A posh restaurant in the West End, London; lunchtime.)

*(*HENRY, *fifties, and his sister,* VANESSA, *early sixties, sit, waiting.)*

VANESSA: You've read his book, haven't you? The new one. It's out. *(Beat)* I saw it in Waterstone's. It's in the window. *(Beat)* I suppose it shall do very well. *(Beat)* Being in the window. *(Short pause)* He's going to ask what you think about his book you know.

HENRY: No, he won't. He's cleverer than that. *(Reaching for the wine bottle)* You are sure you don't want a drink? It might make the play—.

VANESSA: I'd fall asleep, Henry. I shall probably fall asleep anyway, but… *(Laughs)* Theatre has become so…

HENRY: Hasn't it. *(Pouring the wine:)* But you don't mind if I—.

VANESSA: Drink what you like, Henry, I'm not counting,

HENRY: Can I do nothing wrong? *(Beat)* I should be ill more often.

VANESSA: You are not ill. *(Beat)* You are not ill, you are getting better.

HENRY: And if 1 don't—you'll kill me. *(Laughs)* Here he is now.

(SAM, *early fifties, American, approaches their table.*)

SAM: *(Sitting down)* Sorry I'm late. I waited forever for a tube. I hope you haven't—

HENRY: No. No. Sit down. Excuse me for not getting up.

VANESSA: Henry—

HENRY: You've met my sister, Vanessa, haven't you?

SAM: I'm sure we—

VANESSA: With your wife.

HENRY: Hand me your glass.

VANESSA: What an actress. Henry, that's what I was starting to say—what the theatre is missing. She should never have left the stage.

SAM: My wife still acts. She hasn't left—.

VANESSA: *(Not hearing:)* She is missed! Sorely missed. Tell her that for me, will you?

SAM: Actually, she's in a play right—.

VANESSA: *(Not hearing:)* What time is it, dear?

HENRY: You'd better go.

SAM: Go? How late am—?

HENRY: Vanessa just dropped me off. She's seeing—.

VANESSA: Do excuse me for running like this, but you know the theatre, it waits for no one. *(goes to kiss Henry)* I'll pick you up, Henry. Now what theatre was it again?

HENRY: The Phoenix.

VANESSA: Yes. *(Beat)* Yes. That is the one. Sam.

SAM: Vanessa.

VANESSA: Now just don't take your wife away to America. We need her here, Sam. Don't do like you did with poor Richard Burton. *(She leaves.)*

SAM: What did I do to Richard Burton?

(Short pause)

HENRY: *(As he drinks)* She's seeing the matinee of the Tom Howard play.

SAM: Lucky her.

HENRY: Say that again.

(Beat)

SAM: What? I just said—.

HENRY: And I said she's seeing the Tom Howard. And then you said—lucky her.

SAM: So? *(Beat)* What's wrong with—?

HENRY: The last time we talked about Howard—.

SAM: I trashed him, I remember this. *(Beat)* And—. This may come as a surprise to you, Henry, but later I felt quite terrible about what I'd said. I mean, I for one think we should try to be a little more generous to our peers. It isn't an easy thing—writing, we both know that. So why every writer feels the need, almost the obsession, to attack his contemporaries, this I do not know. *(Beat)* And this, I have decided to do something about. *(Beat)* I have vowed that if I do not have something positive to say about a fellow writer then I shall say nothing at all.

HENRY: And this goes for Tom Howard?

SAM: My lips are sealed.

(HENRY and SAM laugh.)

HENRY: I believed you there for a second.

SAM: No you didn't.

HENRY: Really, I was beginning to worry that I was going to have to watch what I said.

SAM: Bullshit. When have we ever watched what we said. How long have we been having these lunches—.

HENRY: I thought—.

SAM: Years, right. I don't remember exactly, but years. And when have we ever watched what we said. *(Beat)* And after three bottles of wine, when have we ever remembered what we said.

(SAM laughs. HENRY laughs.)

SAM: Speaking of—

HENRY: I'll get another bottle. Chardonnay is fine? You know I can't drink red—.

SAM: I'm drinking it, aren't I? So don't ask. *(Short pause)* Which is ours the guy or the girl?

HENRY: It's a guy, but not him.

SAM: A guy though. So that's what I get for being late.

HENRY: I think he's just assigned to this—.

SAM: I was just joking. I didn't mean—.

HENRY: Oh. I— *(Beat)* That's him. *(Beat)* He sees me. *(Pause)* So... *(Beat)* Come on, do I look that bad?

SAM: What do you mean? You look—.

HENRY: At least I'm not dead yet. *(Beat)* Vanessa is taking very good care of me. So I am assured of a slow death. *(Laughs)*

SAM: You look terrific. Really. You do.

(Short pause)

HENRY: Thank you.

SAM: Now who was it that said you'd been looking ill? Somebody was saying that. I'll have to remember who it was and put him straight. You look terrific. *(Pause)*

Have you looked over the menu? *(Beat)* Give me a second then.

(Pause)

HENRY: Your new book is out.

SAM: Uh-huh. *(Beat)* Have-you seen-the jacket? It looks like someone threw up on a book.

(Beat)

HENRY: That should do a lot for sales.

SAM: Tell me about it.

(Pause. Fade out begins:)

SAM: What are you having?

HENRY: The fish here is usually…

(Fade out.)

2.
Sam's adventure of the new book.

(The restaurant. HENRY *and* SAM *are eating their main courses.)*

SAM: I told her that every writer uses what's around him. Where else does he look? *(Beat)* You were right about the salmon.

HENRY: I have never had bad fish here.

SAM: It's a good place to know about.

HENRY: Especially in the West End.

SAM: There's so many—.

HENRY: Aren't there. That's why this place is good to know.

SAM: Funny, I think I've passed it—. I don't know. It's been here for a while?

HENRY: A couple of years at least.

SAM: Amazing. *(Beat)* Anyway… *(Eating:)* Back to Mary.

SAM: And it's not just Mary. I'm telling you this has gotten serious. *(Beat)* Look, I will admit to maybe having been a tiny bit bald about taking from—. Using—. No, it wasn't "using". As I have been saying, where else does a writer look for his ideas? "Using" sounds like "stealing" or something. Plagiarizing, even. *(Beat)* So—: I quote unquote took from people we know. But I have always done that; after twelve novels you would think Mary would understand that. *(Beat)* I need to take it from wherever I can get it. *(Beat)* The stories were just sitting there to incorporate. *(Beat)* I observe life. This is what we do, Henry. That is how I see it. *(Short pause)* And Ben's going to college next year. You can't afford to start getting picky.

HENRY: *(Eating:)* Mary mentioned that. It doesn't seem possible.

SAM: How long did you and Mary talk anyway?

HENRY: We just—.

SAM: Forget it. She's called everyone. You'd think I'd committed some sort of heinous crime against nature. *(Beat)* She married me, after all. *(Short pause)* Look, I don't want to bore—

HENRY: No, please. I've been wanting to hear about what's been going on ever since she phoned —.

SAM: She must have thought that because we were having lunch—.

HENRY: She didn't mention our having lunch.

SAM: No? *(Beat)* She's told everyone, I'm sure. Hell,

(Short pause)

HENRY: I think she called to see how I was doing.

SAM: Of course she did. *(Pause)* Henry, I'm sorry; why I'm—

HENRY: She said Ben wants to go to school in the States.

SAM: Yeh. I don't know why. He'd done the work for Oxford. Do you know why? Did Mary—?

HENRY: No. No, she didn't say.

(Short pause)

SAM: She doesn't talk to me.

HENRY: I gathered. But you can't tell me this is the first time you've used your wife in a story.

SAM: Of course it's not! *(Beat)* Of course. *(Laughs)* And that is my goddamn point, Henry! A million times before. Maybe not so—. So—I don't know, blatant. For Christ sake even her Mother calls from Ohio. So how the hell did she get a copy? Knopf doesn't even publish until the end of the month.

HENRY: How did she?

SAM: *(Realizing:)* Mary sent her bound galleys. That's how!

HENRY: Or maybe the legal department at Knopf, if she's somebody—

SAM: My mother-in-law is nobody. Nobody knows her. Even if she was the character in the bloody book, which I am not saying she is, nobody's ever going to know it. *(Beat)* And I do not make fun. I have fun with this character. You understand that.

HENRY: Sure.

(Short pause)

SAM: Mary. Maybe one or two of her sisters, maybe I put them into the book—as characters. A few things that have happened to them, I have incorporated. Or rather, I have recorded. But I twist these around and use them for my purposes, Henry. I am a writer, after all. I am a novelist. Do they not know this? Do they not realize that this is what I do? *(Beat)* Okay maybe, and just maybe, they are recognizable to one or two close friends or family members or maybe a few other people around the town they live in. So what is the big deal. I would be honored. *(Beat)* And as for her father, he's dead for Christ sake. What's the big deal? He can't be offended. *(Beat)* Him I admit using. Not the mother. Only the father.

HENRY: And he's dead.

SAM: That is right. *(Beat)* But I don't use his name. I change some things. *(Beat)* Why am I on the defensive anyway? That is the question. This is art after all. And you take things from life! And it is in this way—this is what I should have said to her—this is how food has been put on the table for the last twenty-two years. This is how she has been able to keep her artistic integrity working only on plays that quote unquote matter to her, and pay about two pence. What does she think I've been doing all these years writing goddamn fairy tales?!

(Short pause)

HENRY: I say we start on another bottle, don't you?

SAM: I'm not writing today. So why not get plastered.

(SAM *pours.*)

HENRY: Cheers.

SAM: Cheers.

HENRY: Anyway, Sam—to your book. May you have a success despite everything.

SAM: Thanks.

(HENRY *and* SAM *drink.*)

SAM: And to your health, Henry.

HENRY: Despite everything.

(HENRY *and* SAM *drink.*)

(*Awkward pause*)

SAM: Sorry, I keep bumping—

HENRY: These wheelchairs are built rather clunky. I could turn to the side—.

SAM: Please, no. No. Henry, I wasn't saying— *(Beat)* My fault really.

(*Short pause*)

HENRY: It doesn't embarrass me anymore, Sam.

SAM: Why should it ever have? *(Beat)* Anyway about my book…

HENRY: To change the subject.

SAM: That was the subject one minute ago, Henry. *(Beat)* So—. You should have seen the jacket design I wanted. There's this friend of mine, a wonderful designer. He would have done it as a favor really. Books pay nothing compared to—. I don't know. Other stuff. Business-type stuff. He told me what he had in mind. It was great. But Anton said no. I think it sounded too inviting, the idea and god forbid a book should look inviting. *(Beat)* What publishers know about publishing.

HENRY: You could write on the head of a—.

SAM: You want to know what sort of publicity they're giving me? Anton's all hot about this. They are buying a quarter page add in the *Times Supplement*. *(Beat)* When he told me you'd have thought he was handing over a million pounds.

HENRY: Why don't you move—?

SAM: Because I'm loyal!!! *(Beat)* And because everybody's no different. It's bad in New York, but here—. I shouldn't be surprised. I knew what to expect—the moment I first walked into Anton's office—Anton's closet would be more appropriate—whatever they call the place where his publisher keeps Anton, and there on his desk was a manual typewriter. Not a word processor, not an electronic typewriter, not even a goddamn electric. A manual that looks like he'd been given it when he went off to boarding school.

HENRY: Probably was.

SAM: You write. You work. You struggle. And you end up like dust, collecting on a shelf.

HENRY: Are you talking about Anton or—?

SAM: You are supposed to feel good. The book comes out, you have something in you hands that you can touch, that takes up space and you should feel pretty satisfied. At least for a moment or two.

HENRY: It's going to do very well. It's going to be a smash.

SAM: I tell Mary that and she cries. She says she's never going to tell me another secret for as long as she lives. I ask her, what secrets have you told me? I don't remember one secret she's ever told me.

HENRY: She'll get over it. Once you get the reviews. She'll see—.

SAM: The first one was okay.

HENRY: You've already been—?

SAM: Two. *(Beat)* Just two. The first—they got Fred to do it. And Fred has always been good to me. He likes me. *(Beat)* I like him.

HENRY: He's a jerk.

SAM: Not to me. *(Beat)* But it was that asshole on the *Observer*—

HENRY: I missed that. When did—

SAM: Next week. *(Beat)* If critics knew what they did. *(Beat)* What they let loose. *(Beat)* This scumbag starts talking about the wife—right from the beginning he is obsessed with the wife character. He says she's pathetic. In this age of liberation, he takes her apart. Mary needs no more ammunition than that. *(Short pause)* It's not just the reader who reads these things. It's us. We read them. *(Beat)* We read them with our kids around us running and playing—when my kids still ran and played—I do remember this—it used to be really savage. Ben used to cry— "Daddy's got another bad review!" *(Beat)* Of course then I'd have to say— "But Ben, it is not all bad, this gentleman does say a few rather okay things about your Dad's new novel on which he has slaved these past two years. Or rather, Ben, it is the things he has chosen not to say that should give us heart." Like—that he didn't throw up reading it and rip it up and flush it down the toilet. *(Short pause)* So—*The Observer*. Thank you, thank you, thank you.

(Pause)

HENRY: Maybe Mary won't—

SAM: A friend—a quote unquote friend—has already sent a copy to her. She works at this newspaper. *(Beat)* Yesterday morning, at ten a.m., she sent it. I guess she figured she could destroy my whole day that way. Plus of course THE MOTHER phones as well with her unsolicited review. *(Beat)* It is something like six in the morning in Cleveland and she has been up all night reading and crying over my book—and there is not a lot in it that should be sad, Henry. *(Beat)* Yesterday was fun; what a fun fun day it was. *(Beat)* I have a deal with myself not to have a drink before six thirty, do you do that?

HENRY: I used to.

SAM: Except for lunches like this.

HENRY: Because you're not writing.

SAM: Right. *(Short pause)* That rule almost broke me yesterday.

HENRY: I'm sorry.

(Pause)

SAM: *(Sighs, takes a sip of wine)* Anyway, I hear the *Guardian*'s going to be positive. Maybe even better than that; Anton's heard about it, but hasn't seen it, so I think he's being quite cautious with me. *(Beat)* We'll see.

HENRY: I'm sure it'll be—.

SAM: It better. *(Beat)* Please, please, please.

(Pause as HENRY and SAM eat.)

HENRY: *(Finally:)* About Mary's reaction to seeing a character based on herself—.

SAM: A couple of similarities. And the wife isn't the jerk! I'm the jerk. *(Beat)* The husband in the book is the jerk.

HENRY: Right. *(Short pause)* I was going to say that I have had a somewhat similar experience; with Keith and my book, *The Lefthander*.

SAM: Oh yes.

HENRY: You've read it?

SAM: Everyone thinks it's your best book. I love that sort of thing.

HENRY: I wouldn't think it was—. *(Beat)* So I watched Keith as he read it. I had given him the proofs. I made lunch for us and watched this big black gay guy reading my book about this big black gay guy and

EATING WORDS

his—. *(Beat)* Well, you've read the book, right? *(Beat)* It sold like nothing.

SAM: That's not what I heard.

HENRY: It's being reissued with a series of gay novels. Anyway, when Keith finished it, you know what he said? *(Beat)* He said— "Remember what happened to Joe Orton." *(Beat)* That's it. *(Beat)* I still published the book. And Keith forgot about it I guess. Or maybe he even ended up a little flattered. Who knows. *(Laughs to himself)*

SAM: But what you're saying is that you thought Keith was really threatening—?

HENRY: I think he was joking. *(Beat)* The character as you may remember isn't a bad character.

SAM: Neither is the mother-in-law in my book, Henry! *(Beat)* A bit silly maybe, but if you listen to Mary and her sisters talk about their mother—. If I put that sort of thing in—. What I wrote doesn't—. That family should be thanking me. That is what I think. *(Short pause)* Orton's lover didn't kill him because Orton had put him in a play.

HENRY: I didn't mean—.

SAM: He killed him because he was jealous of the success. At least that's certainly the point Lahr was making—.

HENRY: I just meant—. You know. He was trying to threaten. *(Beat)* Keith was. So he chose— *(Beat)* But of course he was only joking. It was like a literary joke. *(Beat)* You know Keith.

SAM: I have to say, not that well, it's usually Mary—. At parties—

HENRY: A lot smarter than you'd at first think. *(Beat)* Reading all the time, Sam. Of course not exactly the type of stuff you or I, you know. But reading. *(Laughs)* Someday I am going to target him as my audience. I'd like to try that. To write for people like him. It'd be interesting to try to write a book that could be published in *The Daily Mail*. *(Laughs)* My books obviously—to him were bullshit. *(Short pause)* A good boy though. He wouldn't have hurt me for…

SAM: Of course not.

(Short pause)

HENRY: What beautiful hair on that boy.

(Beat)

SAM: Sorry!

HENRY: Really, let me move the wheelchair to—.

SAM: I keep bumping.

HENRY: It's no trouble.

(Pause)

SAM: *(Finally:)* You know Jack and Beth.

HENRY: What about them? They aren't—?

SAM: No, no. *(Beat)* They're fine. *(Beat)* It's just that they won't talk to me either. This is according to Mary, of course. They talk to her. *(Beat)* Daily. Maybe hourly. *(Beat)* To—as she puts it— "commiserate".

HENRY: Are they in your book too?

SAM: I wouldn't say that. *(Beat)* Certainly in no way that could ever give offence. I do not use names. I do not use their looks. Just because we took them to our place on Cape Cod—.

HENRY: I didn't know you and Jack and Beth were—

SAM: We aren't. *(Beat)* We aren't close at all. We offered and—. You know. Somehow they accepted. Anyway—.

HENRY: I hear Cape Cod is beautiful.

SAM: You should— *(Beat)* When you have the time. If you're going to be in the States anyway—.

HENRY: Let's talk about that later. We have all afternoon, don't we?

SAM: Yeah. *(Beat)* Goddamn right we do. *(Laughs)* So—Cape Cod. Jack and Beth loved it. They weren't much trouble either. *(Beat)* I thought they would be, especially Jack, but I was pleasantly surprised.

HENRY: Good for Jack.

SAM: So—there's this bit, this very small bit in the novel about this English woman who is visiting Cape Cod and there are one or two things that happen to her—that the narrator actually fantasizes as happening to her. This is what people are not getting that there is fantasy in this book.

HENRY: *(As if quoting:)* A work of the imagination.

SAM: Yeah. Yeah. And so the character has sex with a teenage boy on the beach one night. I made this up. I swear I did. I am not saying Beth had sex with a teenager on the beach. *(Beat)* Where do I ever say that?? *(Beat)* And if she did, Henry, well—I certainly am not supposed to know about it.

(Short pause)

HENRY: And Jack?

SAM: I am told by reliable sources that he would like to hurt me. *(Beat)* But I am also told, Henry, that this has done a lot for their marriage. But do I get credit for that?! No way! *(Beat)* Hell as a couple they were pretty boring. I didn't even give the character a husband. I had no use for their relationship at all.

HENRY: Jack writes. He should understand.

SAM: Essays. That makes it worse. He thinks you use anything there should be footnotes.

HENRY: Maybe in this case you should suggest—

(Laughs)

SAM: Good idea! Serve them right! The literal mindedness. You think I was writing his wife's fucking biography. *(Beat)* Anyway Mary thinks they might sue.

HENRY: How cheap. *(Beat)* What does Anton say?

SAM: I'm waiting to see if Jack has the guts. If he does then I'll tell Anton who will then get sick. *(Beat)* I know my editor. *(Short pause)* Sometimes you have to ask yourself—where is the support? Where are the people who are supposed to be on your side? *(Beat)* You were saying, Henry, you gave Keith the galleys for *The Lefthand*.

HENRY: *Hander.*

SAM: I did the same thing with Mary. This is when it started. *(Beat)* Now this is my wife. This is the person who is supposed to help me. *(Beat)* As she's reading, she keeps looking up at me, biting her lower lip, then sort of twitching her neck like she was cold. *(Beat)* And oh was she ever cold, Henry! *(Beat)* Had I only known. *(Beat)* I watch her close the galleys, and then I say rather cutely— "well?" Big question mark, big question mark. You know how you feel, you're nervous. You're frightened. You try to make a joke— "Pretty bad, huh?" And then she says and I quote, Henry: I hope the warehouse where the, books are kept burns to the ground. I hope all typed copies somehow suddenly mysteriously disappear—if there is a God they will—and finally I pray with all my might that all ten of your fingers atrophy and drop off—hopefully with terrible pain—assuming, that is—that you can still feel pain or any other human emotion—and then this atrocity will go on no longer.

(Pause)

HENRY: I want to read this book.

SAM: It's very funny. Philip Roth wrote me a personal note, he loved it.

HENRY: Well then, he's a writer.

SAM: That's right. *(Beat)* That is right. *(Beat)* So, I laughed when Mary says this. "Atrocity, Mary?" I say "Aren't we a wee bit exaggerating? I mean, the Holocaust was an atrocity." But she goes into the kitchen and I hear her rummaging around in the cabinets. My first thought was that she's going to get a knife.

HENRY: Mary would never—.

SAM: What can I say? So I have a vivid imagination. And I'm thinking—knife. And then I start to think that Anton, my erstwhile editor, will have a field day with my murder. You English may not have any guts but when there's a murder you are great; right in there, routing around. *(Beat)* But she doesn't come out with a knife. She comes out with a package of letters. The letters I had written her when she was still in school.

HENRY: She keeps them in the kitchen?

SAM: That tells you something.

HENRY: Fascinating.

SAM: Isn't it.

HENRY: There's a story there.

SAM: I'm writing it. I was working on it this morning

HENRY: Good.

SAM: And she throws them in my face. *(Short pause)* After she left I started to read them. They're pretty well written.

HENRY: When did Mary actually walk out then?

SAM: It took her forever, Henry. It took weeks. *(Laughs to himself:)* Just like the wife in my novel.

HENRY: Do you know where she is?

SAM: Her sister came—Jean, not Helen who's the one you know. She's the nice one who danced that time with Keith.

HENRY: Helen, I remember her.

SAM: She's back in Boston.

HENRY: Ah.

SAM: Jean's here for something or other.

HENRY: I see.

SAM: So Jean got some of Mary's things this morning. I asked her rather politely where my wife was—and you'd have thought I'd tried to rape her. *(Beat)* I didn't put Jean in the book. In the next one I won't make that mistake again.

(Pause, and the scene begins to fade out.)

SAM: Anyway, I thought I'd go by the play she's in one night—.

HENRY: *(A bit drunk now:)* She's not in the Tom Howard?!

SAM: No, no. *(Beat)* Her? She'd never take a job that pays.

(Fade out)

3.
Henry's tale of courage

(The Restaurant; a while later)

SAM: Sixty thousand dollars? Jesus. And you have to teach what? Twice a week? Three times a week?

HENRY: There'll be two seminars. I could do them both in one day, I suppose.

SAM: One day a week for sixty thousand dollars. Where'd you hear about this job? How come I never hear about these jobs?

HENRY: They called me. Through a friend of a friend. *(Beat)* I guess at some party or whatever sometime I said—in the abstract, that I'd like to spend time in the States. That I like to teach. And two plus two and so forth. *(Beat)* I guess. *(Beat)* No one's actually told me how my name—.

WAITER: Excuse me. Would you like coffee? Dessert?

HENRY: A coffee for me I think.

SAM: The same.

HENRY: And what about a whiskey? Two Jamisons?

SAM: I've got nothing to do today.

WAITER: Two Jamisons.

(WAITER *goes.*)

(Short pause)

SAM: What does your doctor say? The winters are very cold in Upstate New York.

HENRY: My doctor says I can do anything I want. Go anywhere I want. *(Beat)* Drink anything I want.

SAM: You've got to give me the name of this doctor. *(Laughs)* What does Keith say? He must be very excited.

HENRY: Sure. *(Beat)* Yes.

(Long pause)

SAM: What about housing? Do they have a place—

HENRY: I figure I shall just rent a flat. It couldn't be—.

SAM: No, no, get them to give you some housing help. They expect that. So negotiate for it. *(Beat)* They expect it, but it is up to you to ask. *(Beat)* They own houses. You could get a whole house. *(Beat)* It's worth asking about, Henry.

(Pause)

HENRY: New scenery. The change. *(Suddenly energized:)* To me it is all about pushing all the crap away for a while and getting back to what really matters, Sam!! *(Beat)* There is so much crap. One only wants to get on with it. *(Beat)* So one tries to find a new space; someplace with life in it. What she has done to this country, Sam.

SAM: The States are no—.

HENRY: There, I wouldn't care. I wouldn't have to. *(Beat)* You understand that. *(Beat)* I think that in someplace different I could be alone. In a way, I guess that's what I'm looking for. Ever since I was in school I thought that that was what being a writer was all about. That that was the attraction, Sam. That was what being an artist means.

SAM: To be by yourself?

HENRY: To follow your own thoughts—you know—and dreams. To discover! *(Beat)* To discover. *(Beat)* And leave other people to do the other things.

SAM: That is attractive. Sure.

(Pause)

HENRY: You know last summer Keith and I got a cottage on Jura. The Hebrides. *(Beat)* Pretty much the same place as George Orwell had when he was writing *Nineteen Eighty-Four*.

SAM: You're not sure?

HENRY: It might have been. *(Beat)* It probably was. *(Beat)* The nights were as peaceful as anything I've ever experienced And the people—. Call me strange but I like the Scots. I really don't think they're so gloomy. *(Beat)* My agent, George Hopewell—

SAM: I know George.

HENRY: He came up for a few days and went fishing.

(Short pause)

SAM: The whole things sounds ideal, Henry.

HENRY: To me. *(Beat)* To you. *(Beat)* Being isolated from the world does not frighten us. *(Beat)* We live for it, in a way, don't we? *(Beat)* Keith left after four days. He said he had started to listen to the blood flow through his head. I told to see a doctor. One or two crazy things he did—. *(Beat)* You don't want to know. *(Beat)* So—Keith left. Or for a while I thought he'd drowned. He had said nothing to me. I was a wreck of course. 1 got no work done. Not a lick, Sam. *(Beat)* Oh well. *(Beat)* He came back to London is what he did. I'd forgotten I'd given him a set of keys to the flat. So he was happy. He had a friend visit with him while I was gone.

(Pause)

SAM: So at least he was safe.

HENRY: *(Laughs to himself)* I suppose so. *(Short pause)* So George came up to hold my hand and he went fishing while I pretended to write.

(Beat)

WAITER: Two Jamisons?

HENRY: Thank you.

SAM: Thanks.

(Pause as HENRY *and* SAM *sip.)*

HENRY: A brilliant fly fisherman, George. When he retires that's what he's going to do.

SAM: How old is he now anyway?

HENRY: George? *(Beat)* I don't know. Seventy? Who knows. *(Short pause)* But anyway the whole summer wasn't a complete loss. I did start to read Orwell again. What an extraordinary man. I've already planned him as the first subject of my public lectures at Cornell.

SAM: You have to give—?

HENRY: Two. One in the Fall. One in the Spring, To show me off. For sixty thousand dollars they need something to show off. *(Beat)* But I can choose. *(Short pause)* What I'd like to concentrate on is the man's courage. He gives us all strength today. Or he should at least. He certainly does me. *(Beat)* You know of course he was dying when he wrote *Nineteen Eighty-Four*. He knew it too. He tried to hide it. *(Beat)* He could even joke about it. And he certainly denied it when he was asked. *(Beat)* When someone was crude enough to ask. *(Beat)* Or cared enough to ask. *(Beat)* In fact I have a thesis that I plan to propose that the wisdom of this great book derives in part from the fact that he was dying. *(Beat)* You feel that somehow. *(Beat)* A dying man's last cry. But a cry that is not about himself, but about his world. That is where the real courage is. That is the heroism. *(Beat)* At such a point to think about the world. *(Beat)* To care about what happens. *(Pause)* I should tell you, Sam—Keith, he died last week.

SAM: Henry, I—?!

HENRY: I just found out myself yesterday.

SAM: Oh shit. Henry—

HENRY: His mother flew in from Jamaica to take care of him. *(Beat)* She wouldn't let me see him. *(Beat)* Or near him. *(Beat)* We talked once on the phone about four weeks ago. *(Short pause)*

The Irish know how to make whiskey, don't they?

SAM: Henry, I'm sorry. Mary didn't—

HENRY: She doesn't know. As I said, I found out just last night. And I guess it still hasn't sunk in. He was a beautiful man, Sam. *(Beat)* A gentle man. *(Beat)* I loved him very very much. *(Pause)* So— *(Sighs)* I haven't of course been officially offered the Cornell job. There have only been letters... *(Beat)* I meet next month with a gentleman from the school. Though I expect...

SAM: Pro forma.

HENRY: Why shouldn't it be? *(Beat)* Though no one there has actually seen me. *(Beat)* Perhaps I'll be out of the wheelchair by then.

(Pause)

SAM: Do you know if there was a funeral?

HENRY: I don't know, Sam.

(Short pause)

SAM: Who called you?

HENRY: I think it was his brother. *(Beat)* I think. He didn't say. *(Pause. With sudden energy:)* Orwell I think needed this knowledge of his dying to make his book. *(Beat)* It gave him the clarity. Do you understand?!

SAM: I think—.

HENRY: And so in this sense—in dying he gave us the gift of his vision. Sam, he died to help us all see. To help us know. To help us stop what he could see in his death was happening to the world! *(Beat. Very passionate now:)* Art can do that! *(Beat)* Words can!

(Pause, then:)

(Fade out)

4.
The search for a new inn

(A short while later; SAM *pushes* HENRY *in his wheelchair through the noisy crowded streets of the West End. This, quite a change from the soft whispers of the restaurant.* HENRY *and* SAM *are fairly drunk by now.)*

HENRY: I think it's up here.

SAM: *(To a passerby:)* Excuse me. Excuse… Sorry.

HENRY: Off a little street. *(Beat)* It's the only decent pub around here. There's a room in the back that's usually fairly quiet.

SAM: No darts. *(Beat)* Please, I do not like sitting in a room and dodging darts while I drink. Why this is such a British tradition—.

HENRY: Here! Turn here!

SAM: *(To passersby:)* Excuse us. Please. Watch it. *(Beat)* Move please. *(Beat)* We're trying— *(Beat)* Could you—?! Get out of the way for Christ sake! The man's in a wheelchair!!!

(Obviously the crowd has moved)

SAM: Thank you. Thank you! You're very kind, all of you!

(Short pause as they continue)

HENRY: You should have pushed Rocinante right at them. That's what my sister does.

SAM: Rocinante? It has a name? *(Beat)* Henry, you named your wheelchair Rocinante?

HENRY: Is something wrong with that?

SAM: No, no. *(Laughs)*

HENRY: Why is that funny?

SAM: It's just—. Then for this afternoon at least, then that should make me—.

HENRY: You are much too skinny for my idea of Sancho Panza, Sam. *(Beat)* Much. *(Beat)* But if that is who you wish to be, I shall not stand in your way. This decision I leave up to you. There! That's the pub there!!! *(To passersby:)* Get out of the way!!!

(Fade out)

5.
The Knight Errant and Sancho encounter an ugly vision.

(The back room of a very crowded and noisy pub. HENRY is at a table, waiting for SAM to get drinks from the bar. A YOUNG WOMAN sits very close to HENRY, crowded in at the next table.)

YOUNG WOMAN: Excuse me, is someone using that ashtray?

HENRY: What? No. We don't—. I used to, but— *(Beat)* Please. Take it. It's yours. *(Beat)* Here. *(Beat)* Smoke doesn't bother me. Really.

SAM: *(Approaching the table:)* Sorry. I thought people worked in the afternoon. Could you move in please. *(Beat)* I'm not that skinny. Thank you. *(Beat. To HENRY:)* Jesus. No Jamison, but they had Bushmills.

HENRY: Oh that's fine. Bushmills is fine, Sam.

(HENRY and SAM are both quite a bit drunk by now.)

SAM: Anyway—. *(He sits.)* Cheers.

HENRY: Cheers.

SAM: You feel okay?

HENRY: This'll help. *(Drinks)*

SAM: I feel great. I really feel great.

HENRY: I thought it'd be quieter!

SAM: It's fine. Really. It's great.

HENRY: This young woman here borrowed our ashtray.

YOUNG WOMAN: What? You want it back?

SAM: No, no. *(Beat)* No. Of course not. Our compliments. *(Laughs)* They really do pack them in here. Anyway— *(Short pause)* Henry, I was thinking how funny it was going to be; me in England, you in America. *(Beat)* Me in your country, you in—

HENRY: I understood what you were saying.

SAM: It's like they've chased us both away.

HENRY: You're right. That is exactly what they've done. And don't for a minute kid yourself, that has been their goal all along. If they get rid of people like us... Us...

SAM: I know. I know.

HENRY: You take the artist out of his society, either by force or— *(Beat)* The way they've done it to us, Sam. The way they've done it to you and the way they are doing it to me. Then who is left to stop them? Who is left to stand up and say "J'accuse! J'accuse!" *(Beat)* You see what I am saying.

SAM: Uh-huh. What you say, it—. For me—. You are touching something.... *(Beat)* I've been away from home for eleven long years, Henry. I took my wife. I took my kids. *(Beat)* My wife came home; she's English, but my kids. But me? You know I wonder—. You see what happened and I wonder—. And you too at Cornell, you too will wonder, Henry, watching the news, following what is happening in your own country from afar; from—a great, great distance, Henry. And you wonder—. At least I do. *(Beat)* What if

I had stayed in America? Could I have helped? Could I have changed things? It is a mess there, Henry.

HENRY: Ugly!

SAM: An ugly mess. And it will get worse before it gets better.

HENRY: That is always the way.

SAM: *(Suddenly energized:)* What could I have done? What could I have written that—? What? What? *(Beat)* Hmmmmmmm.

(Pause. Pub noise)

HENRY: I think—and I am not even sure I believe this myself, but for the sake of argument, Sam—I think the artist today—in today's world—is given too much responsibility.

SAM: I do not agree at all! Henry, if anything

HENRY: Let me finish! *(Beat)* Okay? *(Beat)* I think—but I am not saying I believe this—.

SAM: Right.

HENRY: I think, if one would simply let the artist today alone, not pick apart his work…Or her work… Do this for some time. I don't know how long. But to give him time to breathe, you understand. Let the dust settle. We should be working for the future, Sam, writing about what is immortal, for Christ sake, about what doesn't change, not what does, Sam, not what can. *(Beat)* But then again—.

SAM: Exactly, if someone comes along and takes your pen out of your hand and says you cannot write anymore, I forbid it. Well—. Well—. As soon as you get your pen back, you think you're going not to write about that? You have no choice. It is now part of your daily life. Your experience. Is it not? *(Beat)* Things have become all... Twisted together. Like knots. *(Pause)* So you pick up your pen—.

HENRY: Or sit in front of your typewriter. Whatever.

SAM: Yeah, and you ask yourself—if you are honest, you ask yourself, Henry: who am I writing this for? What do I want this to accomplish? And that of course is death, isn't it?

HENRY: Positively.

SAM: But what choice is there? *(Beat)* I guess what I'm saying is that I agree with you. After all that. *(Laughs)* I'm agreeing with something you said a little while ago. What was that you said?

HENRY: When did I say this?

SAM: A short time ago. *(Short pause)* Anyway, I agree. At first I disagreed and now I agree. *(Short pause)* I feel I was a coward to leave my country.

HENRY: You are being very hard—.

SAM: A coward.

HENRY: If you think that, then go—.

SAM: Mary hates New York. Even with a green card she does. *(Beat)* The only auditions she gets is for Shaw plays. She hates Shaw plays.

HENRY: I thought Mary left you.

SAM: She'll come back. She's angry that's all. She'll forget about the book. It is only a book. *(Short pause)* They are scared of us, Henry!!

(SAM *has shouted this, pub noise quiets for a moment as people turn towards him; then noise picks up again.)*

SAM: *(Continued:)* That's how you know that you matter, because they're scared of you. *(Beat)* They put us in jail, don't they? All over the world they do this.

HENRY: You've never been put into jail.

SAM: And why is that? Why? *(Beat)* Because—I am not in my own country.

HENRY: That's not why. It's because you aren't a threat, Sam—as a writer you aren't a threat. Look at what you write about. What I write about. Your books are about living in the world today; about marriages, about divorces, about people with anxieties, sex—.

SAM: I write about more than—!

HENRY: What do you write that could get you thrown into jail?! *(Beat)* Me too! I'm not just saying you! *(Short pause)* What do I write about? I write about a world that is cold to people like me.

SAM: My world is cold and unfeeling and—.

HENRY: So we write the obvious. So you think we should be shot for that? *(Beat)* That we could be shot for that?! *(Beat)* I write love stories.

SAM: Gay love stories. Now in England today—.

HENRY: Don't tell me about England today!!!!

(Pause. Pub noise)

SAM: So—you are running away.

HENRY: I am not running away. I am getting away.

(Short pause)

SAM: Why do we hate our countries? Why do we abandon our homes? *(Beat)* Hmmmmmmm. Makes you sad when you put it that way. *(Short pause)* If I had only stayed think about what I could have done.

HENRY: Stop saying that.

SAM: I could have changed things, Henry.

HENRY: You couldn't have done shit! Who does shit?

SAM: Alexander Solzhenitsyn, he did shit, Henry.

HENRY: You are not Solzhen—.

SAM: Than take Updike! *(Beat)* One wonders if you'd grab him and shake him and say—put into your books what you think our country could be! Fight for it! Use your art, John! Instead of only pointing out anxiety—.

HENRY: If you're talking propaganda—.

SAM: I'm saying—do we have a choice anymore?!!! *(Beat. Louder:)* Do you?!!!!! *(Beat)* Being gay! In your case, being gay. In England. In my case, believing in a society that takes responsibility for itself, for its people, which helps—.

HENRY: Sam—

SAM: It seems to me you'd have to do something!!!

HENRY: I am. I'm going to—.

SAM: *(Yells:)* Why???!!!!!!

HENRY: *(Yells back:)* To write!!!!!!! Goddamnit, to write what I know. *(Beat)* As much as I know. *(Beat)* Honesty—not politics. Truth—not agendas. That's how we change the world.

(The pub is almost silent now; as all have listened to this last shouted exchange. Pause)

YOUNG WOMAN: Excuse me. But I couldn't help overhearing

SAM: What—?

YOUNG WOMAN: You're both some sort of writer, I take it.

SAM: What do you want?

YOUNG WOMAN: What do you write—mysteries? Novels?

SAM: Novels.

(Beat)

YOUNG WOMAN: Well, I know it's none of my business, but your whole conversation seems to me to be, well... It's bull, isn't it?

SAM: Who asked—.

YOUNG WOMAN: I mean, you keep talking about how a writer matters—or maybe it's what he writes that matters. I don't think you have the distinction very clear in your minds, by the way. But that is a minor point. *(Beat)* So how do you matter? Would you like an objective opinion?

SAM: Henry, who is this woman?

YOUNG WOMAN: First, let me remind you that is this 1989, gentlemen. And this is the real world.

(Pub bas been listening and suddenly cheers with this last line.)

YOUNG WOMAN: Try to keep your applause until the end, please. *(Beat)* So, you are an American, I gather.

SAM: That's right.

YOUNG WOMAN: Then I would have thought that you'd at least know better. But I take it you've been away for some time so that will explain it.

SAM: Explain what?

YOUNG WOMAN: I was in San Diego once, just last year for a sales conference and let me tell you I had the time of my life. The weather—I could live there forever! But it wasn't just sunshine and sand that got me—there was a spirit in the air. Call it whatever: an energy, American confidence, whatever, but it was there and it was beautiful, let me tell you. *(Beat)* What Ronald Reagan has accomplished... The world should be on its knees in thanks and I do not exaggerate. That man is a hero. *(Beat)* There is a sense of freedom in your country that you feel in an instant. An entrepreneurial freedom that has given hope to all of us really. After all it is what we are trying to achieve in England now. *(Beat)* In part of England now. *(Beat)* It is a very exciting; time, isn't it? *(Beat)* But I digress. Getting back to you two. To you two writers, to you two 'intellectuals'.

SAM: I didn't say we were—

YOUNG WOMAN: Bull. Any more bullshit from you and we'll all start floating out of here. If I called you an intellectual, you'd be flattered, right?

SAM: Sure. Of course, I—

YOUNG WOMAN: So obviously what you are not aware of is that this word has come to be used today only pejoratively. Am I right?

(Crowd in pub yells agreement.)

YOUNG WOMAN: It's come to mean what? Bullshiter, right? The sort of guys who sit on their asses and talk all day as if talking ever mattered for shit, ever changed anything.

SAM: Look, I don't agree.

YOUNG WOMAN: Oh, now he wants to argue!

*(*YOUNG WOMAN *laughs, others laugh.)*

YOUNG WOMAN: Look, I'm in the real world, okay? You want to know what that is? Listen to what I did today. *(Beat)* I'm trying to sell this Japanese guy this boat. This is lunch. For him it's going to cost about what an okay breakfast costs in Tokyo, I'm talking about the boat not the lunch. *(She laughs.)* He's just been transferred here and he's got to buy something, and I've got this boat or my company does. *(Beat)* Full kitchen, microwave, color T V. A big goddamn boat. This is my assignment. Why? Because I speak Japanese? Are you kidding? It's because I've got the biggest breasts in the company. And rumor has it—

which by the way I now think is true—so the word is that these Japanese like 'em big breasted, sort of a novelty for them I guess. *(Beat)* In the office, we had a whole meeting over whether I'd wear a bra or not. This company is thorough. *(Beat)* So today we have lunch. The boat he buys before we've even ordered. By coffee, he's in such a good mood he takes the whole company and I'm made Vice President. *(Beat)* I think it's Vice President. The interpreter had his mouth full when he told me. Maybe it's President. I don't know. *(Beat)* Some main course, huh? *(She laughs.)* And there you have the real world.

(Some applause from the crowd)

YOUNG WOMAN: Now don't get me wrong; I think I disserve this promotion, whatever it is. I worked hard for it. I arrived on time at the restaurant. I laughed at two very confusing jokes translated from the Japanese. *(Beat)* I laughed before one was even translated. *(Beat)* No. I earned this. I certainly did. And just as soon as my former bosses are given the old heave-ho, as they say in San Diego, I'm going back there and claim my rightful office, be it the President's or the Vice President's. But if it is the latter, then you can all bet your bottom dollar—or pound—on what position I'll be gunning for next week.

(Some applause, then people are coming up to the YOUNG WOMAN *and offering her congratulations, a job well done, nice work, etc.)*

(Fade out)

6.
The encounter in the inn is left far behind

(St James Park; late afternoon. SAM *pushes* HENRY *in the wheelchair. Birdsong, some traffic noise in the distance, but the sense of quiet and peace after the pub.)*

SAM: Did that really happen?

HENRY: What?

SAM: In the pub. That woman. Those people applauding and congratulating her.

HENRY: I couldn't hear. It was too noisy.

SAM: Oh. *(Beat)* You didn't hear?

HENRY: I'm drunk, what about you?

SAM: Is there any other way to be?

(Short pause)

HENRY: Anyway, they say that satellite photos show a quarter or something of the whole Amazon jungle is on fire. *(Beat)* Or been burned up already. *(Beat)* Not quite a quarter. That can't be.

SAM: Whatever.

HENRY: The destruction, it's—. Imagine. *(Beat)* You can't picture it. It's like some global death wish is upon us, Sam. Things are bad. Wherever you look. *(Short pause)* So the idea for the story is about some peasants. I haven't thought this through. I haven't let myself. I know I'll never write it. *(Beat)* Peasants, and I do a kind of thing Golding has done. Even if it does Sound pretentious.

SAM: So you risk it. We risk pretentiousness every day.

HENRY: The peasants, they're not from the jungle. They have escaped to there; refugees say from a revolution.

SAM: Very *Lord Of The Flies*.

HENRY: To a point. *(Beat)* Maybe. I don't know. Yes, but different. *(Beat)* So we start by liking these people. They're peasants; poor, they've run from the fascists. They're here to build a new life for themselves in the Amazon jungle.

SAM: The revolution was a right-wing revolution?

HENRY: That's right.

SAM: *(Stopping the wheelchair)* Henry. Over there,

HENRY: The man or the woman?

SAM: The swans, Henry.

HENRY: I never understood the attraction in feeding swans. You stand in their shit, throwing them food you'd otherwise throw out. The poetic justice of this I get, but where is the joy?

SAM: I'll keep pushing. Giddy-up Rocinante.

HENRY: If you want to rest—. Let's find a bench. We've passed a million empty benches. For some reason St. James Park doesn't have the drawing power of the pubs we've been in.

SAM: I'd rather keep walking.

HENRY: If you wish. *(Beat)* Lead on, I am in your hands, Sancho. *(Short pause)* Of course I've never been to the Amazon. Or any jungle for that matter. So for details I figure I'd end up a little stuck.

SAM: There are books.

HENRY: Still. One wouldn't have the experience—. I mean Kew Gardens is not really very close, is it? *(Beat)* Anyway, as we are talking about books we shall never write—. *(Beat)* My peasants settle in the jungle. But what do they know about jungles? Nothing, Sam. So the first thing they do is try to change it. They begin to clear the land. Literally start burning down everything. This is the only way they know how to survive.

SAM: By destroying?

HENRY: That's what it looks like. They are actually trying to create fields, but from the distance of a satellite, it looks like wanton destruction. *(Short pause)* Now a team of Western conservationists—good people—journey into this jungle. *(Beat)* They tell the peasants that without the vegetation of jungles like these—and there aren't many left for Christ sake—the world needs the oxygen the jungles give off. They create the necessary atmosphere for human life. *(Beat)* The peasants listen but they are thinking: what about us? How do we eat? *(Beat)* The conservationists promise a massive amount of help—both food and technical advice. *(Beat)* At last the peasants give in and stop the burning. The world is saved. At least from this and at least for now. *(Beat)* As for the peasants, the food and help never reaches them; the government won't allow it; and now without the fires, the government soldiers venture into the jungle and either kill or arrest all the peasants. *(Beat)* And that's the end. *(Beat)* Of course I'll never write it.

SAM: Because you've never been to a jungle?

HENRY: Because—it is too Goddamn despairing. *(Short pause)* Total despair may indeed be what I'm feeling. *(Beat)* For us. For our countries. *(Beat)* Certainly for my country. *(Beat)* But it isn't what I want to be expressing, What I need to express. *(Beat)* And that's hope, Sam. Even if it's but some modicum of hope, still that's what we need to be saying, isn't it? *(Beat)* That is what is needed. *(Beat)* When you know that you're dying, you don't want to be told that you're dead.

(Long pause; as they pass by the pond. Swans cry out.)

HENRY: So what's your—?

SAM: I don't have—.

HENRY: Come on. Come on.

(Short pause)

SAM: I've got one that is also set in the jungle.

(A bird cries out.)

HENRY: Bullshit. Come on.

SAM: I'm serious. I do. I even started to write it once.

HENRY: If you're pulling my—

SAM: I'm not!! *(Short pause)* The main character's a painter. American. And what he paints is flowers and fauna of the jungle. *(Beat)* I'm getting thirsty, aren't you?

HENRY: Go toward the river. I think I know an off-license.

(Short pause)

SAM: This painter, he spends months alone in the jungle painting his pictures. He's one of those artists who have removed themselves from the world. *(Beat)* Or rather that is what I want the reader to first think, that the bloke is rather in another world. Nice guy, sure, but—not like you or me. *(Beat)* But then we start to see that his pictures, besides being beautiful in their own right—and I am not underestimating this—besides their beauty, we see what they actually accomplish: with these pictures he has discovered flowers that the world hasn't even known existed, including one that blooms only once and this only in the middle of the night, in a jungle full of snakes and poisonous spiders. He has seen such a flower and he has painted it. *(Beat)* Painted it for the whole world, you could say. *(Beat)* So this painter then is also a discoverer, isn't he? *(Short pause)* And on the other hand, as you have said about the jungle, so much is being destroyed now, this painter then is also recording for the future what we have already killed. *(Beat)* He is preserving life. He is reminding us what we once had. *(Beat)* He is a conscience then. In a way, he is. *(Pause)* Just by painting flowers. *(Laughs to himself)* Of course, he'd never say that about himself. He'd say, he paints what's in front of him, what strikes him as interesting or beautiful or fascinating And that most of his time is involved in the minutiae of that work,: choosing colors, learning about new paints, canvases that don't wrinkle in the jungle humidity. *(Short pause)* And if you were to get him talking about how he sees what he does, you'd end up hearing about what he thinks of other painters, about getting money for his journeys, about the difficulties of travel, what he likes to eat, the flies, the snakes, where to buy boots. *(Pause)* That's it. That's as far as I've ever gotten with this story. *(Pause)* But I've never been to a jungle either. So I better stick to what I know..

(Short pause)

HENRY: Like marriage.

SAM: Why not.

HENRY: Or trips to Cape Cod with English friends. *(Beat)* Wives and lost love letters.

SAM: The difficulties of living in another's country.

(Beat)

HENRY: Tom Howard's plays.

(Beat)

SAM Where to buy comfortable walking shoes.

HENRY: You haven't even mentioned walking shoes.

SAM: I didn't think you'd be interested, Henry.

(As HENRY *and* SAM *stroll:)*

(Fade out)

7.
Upon a bridge comfort is found

(Westminster Bridge)

(The sound of buses and cars going by is heard throughout, sometimes even drowning out what is being said; also boat horns in the distance and once or twice a train.)

(Pause)

*(*HENRY *is alone in his wheelchair.* SAM *hurries from a distance.)*

SAM: *(Calls:)* There you are!

*(*SAM *runs.)*

SAM: How'd you get this far out?

HENRY: I wheeled myself. We can do that, you know.

SAM: When you weren't by the steps, I thought you'd—

HENRY: Did you find the off-license?

(Beat)

SAM: Yeah. Here. We're back to Jamison.

HENRY: I won't complain.

(Pause; they drink out of the bottle.)

SAM: Quite the view.

HENRY: *(Begins to recite Mathew Arnold's* Dover Beach, *making a few small mistakes:)*
"The sea is calm to-night.
The tide is full, the moon lies fair
Upon the Straits; —on the French coast, the light
Gleams, and is gone; the cliffs of England stand.
Glimmering and vast, out in the tranquil bay.
Come to a window, sweet is the night air!
Only, from the long line of spray
Where the ebb meets the moon-blanch'd sand.
Listen! you hear a grating roar

Of pebbles which the waves suck back, and fling.
At their return, up the high strand.
Begin, and cease, and then again begin.
With tremulous cadence slow, and bring
The eternal sadness in.

Sophocles long ago
Heard it on the Aegaean, and this brought
Into his mind a turbid ebb then flow
Of human misery; we
Find also in the sound a thought.
Hearing it by this distant northern sea."

(Cars and buses keep going by)

HENRY: "The sea of faith
Was once, too, at the full, and round earth's shore
Lay like folds of some bright girdle furl'd;
But now I only hear
Its melancholy, long, withdrawing roar.
Retreating to the breath
Of the night-wind down the vast edges drear
And naked shingles of the world.

Ah, love, let us be true
To one another! for the world, which seems
To lie before us like a land of dreams,
So various, so beautiful, so new.
Hath really neither joy, nor love, nor light.
Nor certitude, nor peace, nor help for pain;
And we are here as on a darkling plain
Swept with confused alarms of struggle and flight.
Where ignorant armies clash by night."
(Pause) That's pretty close, but don't quote me. *(Laughs)*
But not bad after thirty-five years. Amazing what stays in you head.

SAM: What grows in your head.

(Beat)

HENRY: What you find in your head and begin to understand.

(Short pause; bus goes by.)

HENRY: It's not Dover Beach, but the Thames will do.

(Short pause)

SAM: Now how about "Westminster Bridge", since that's rather appropriate, considering where we are standing.

HENRY: Sorry. Never had to learn it. *(Beat)* Don't know it. *(Takes bottle and drinks)* Cheers. *(Short pause)* Are we drunk again yet?

SAM: I think we must be.

HENRY: Good.

(Pause; then SAM hands HENRY a bag.)

SAM: Here.

HENRY: *(Opening the bag)* Is this what you've been carrying. I thought it looked like a book.

SAM: I bought it for you, Henry. That's why I was late. *(Beat)* It was in a window... *(Beat)* I had no trouble getting a tube, I just stopped when I saw...

(Short pause)

HENRY: This I doubt. Not about stopping, but that you bought this for me.

SAM: Henry—

HENRY: That doesn't mean I won't take it, Sam. *(Beat)* I'm taking it. *(Short pause)* Thank you. *(He has opened the book, it is an early edition of Walt Whitman's* Leaves Of Grass. *He has opened to* A Song of Joys.*)*
"O to make the most jubilant song!
Full of music—full of manhood, womanhood, infancy!"
(Beat) I wonder if Clause 28 can ban public readings of

Walt Whitman. *(Short pause)* Here. You read some. It's better in an American accent.

(SAM *takes the book.*)

SAM: It's an early printing of the 1892 deathbed edition.

HENRY: I know, I know.

(Short pause)

(SAM *begins to read sections of* A Song Of Joys; *as he does buses cars, people pass them on the bridge, often drowning out what is being read.)*

SAM: *(Reading:)*
"O for the voices of animals—O for the swiftness and
   balance of fishes!
O for the dropping of raindrops in a song!
O for the sunshine and motion of waves in a song!'

O the joy of my spirit—it is uncaged—it darts like
   lightning!
It is not enough to have this globe or a certain time,
I will have thousands of globes and all time.

O the engineer's joys! to go with a locomotive!
To hear the hiss of steam, the merry shriek, the steam-
   whistle, the laughing locomotive!
To push with resistless way and speed off in the
distance."

(The harbor, bridge are alive with sound—buses, cars, people, trains. Big Ben, etc)

SAM: "O to go back to the place where I was born.
To hear the birds sing once more.
To ramble about the house and barn and over the fields
   once more.
And through the orchard and along the old lanes once
   more.
O to bathe in the swimming-bath, or in a good place
   along shore.

To splash the water! To walk ankle-deep, or race naked
  along the shore.
O to realize space!
The plenteousness of all, that there are no bounds.
  To emerge and be of the sky, of the sun and moon and
  flying clouds, as one with them."

(SAM *turns a page and finds another section.*)

SAM: "O to sail to sea in a ship!
To leave this steady unendurable land,
To leave the tiresome sameness of the streets, the
  sidewalks and the houses,
To leave you O you solid motionless land, and entering
  a ship. To sail and sail and sail!"

(*Pause. Harbor and bridge noise.* SAM *hands* HENRY *back the book.*)

SAM: Here.

HENRY: Thank you. I will cherish it for as long as I live. (*Short pause*) What do you want to do now?

SAM: I don't know. (*Beat*) There are some book stalls on the South Bank.

HENRY: The ones by the National Theatre?

SAM: Yeah. They're not much—.

HENRY: They're not that bad. What the hell. What's the harm in having a look, I always say. (*Beat*) Unless you have to—

SAM: No. (*Beat*) I have no where I want to go.

HENRY: Good.

(HENRY *and* SAM *begin to go across the bridge.*)

HENRY: You want a drink?

SAM: Sure. Thanks.

(SAM *drinks. Train goes by.*)

SAM: *(As they go; to a passersby:)* Excuse us. Sorry. *(Beat)* Watch it. Sorry. *(Beat)* Could you move please. Thank you.

(Pause)

HENRY: You know, when I die, it's not people I'll miss, it's their words.

(Pause, HENRY *and* SAM *go, leaving only traffic noise behind them, which finally—)*

(Fades out)

END OF PLAY

ADVICE TO EASTERN EUROPE

ADVICE TO EASTERN EUROPE was first broadcast on B B C Radio 3 on 27 December 1990. The cast was as follows:

PAUL	Colin Stinton
HELENA	Edita Brychta
PETER	Simon Treves
GERALD	Oliver Cotton
RECEPTIONIST	Tara Dominick
CLERK	Joanna Myers
WAITER	Andrew Wincott
BUSKER	John Bull
READER	Jenny Howe
Director	Ned Chaillet

CHARACTERS & SETTING

PAUL, *twenty-seven, American, working as a script reader for* PETER, *a producer/film distributor.*

HELENA LAMICOVA, *twenty-seven, Czech, screenwriter, and daughter of internationally famous Czech film director.*

PETER, *English, producer / film distributor with his office on Wardour Street, Soho.*

GERALD, *early forties, American though with a strong British accent; screenwriter and teacher.*

WAITRESS

WAITER

Others

The play takes place in London, today.

1.

(An office in a building on Wardour Street, London. A discussion is going on between an English man and a woman with a Czech accent; what is being said cannot be made out.)

PAUL: *(Quietly, to us:)* I haven't said a word since she's come in. *(Beat)* Actually Peter asked me to come into his office and she was here. He wanted me to meet her. And there she was. *(Beat)* Sitting. *(Beat)* There. *(Beat)* I don't even know what she does in the film business in Prague. An actress I would suppose. By the look—. The way she—. She's very confident. Sitting. There. *(Beat)* I suppose I'll find out. That's why Peter—. He must have had a reason. I don't think I've heard a single word anyone has said. *(Laughs to himself)* We're about the same age. She's in her twenties I'm sure she's in her twenties, Notice how she doesn't look you in the eye. She hasn't looked me in the eye. It's like I don't even exist. Who am I? *(Laughs to himself)* She's hardly bothered to notice me. To her I'm just the fellow who keeps pouring the tea. *(Beat)* And offering. Offering.

(Office discussion gets louder.)

PAUL: *(To others:)* Anyone want more tea?

PETER: You just asked us that, Paul.

HELENA: No. But thank you.

PETER: Pretty soon it'll be time for a drink. What time do you have, Paul?

PAUL: It's...I don't have a watch.

HELENA: Five. It is five.

PETER: What time do you start to drink in Prague?

HELENA: Whenever we feel we wish to.

(Laughter)

PETER: Sounds just like the B B C!

(Laughter)

PAUL: Sounds just like the—. *(Stops himself. To us:)* That was my joke! *(Beat To* HELENA*:)* That is where you should also go. To the B B C. In fact, there are one or two names—friends of mine—who—.

HELENA: I was already there.

(Short pause)

PETER: She was at the B B C just yesterday. She's been telling us all about it, Paul.

PAUL: Of course. Of course, she has! *(Laughs)* Sorry. I don't know where my.... I'm going to have a biscuit. *(He takes a biscuit and starts eating.)*

HELENA: *(To* PETER*:)* What I did not tell you is that, the secretary—the one who came to get me—I think she was a secretary, not only did we get lost getting to the office, but we went through these two doors...

(Fade out of discussion until it is in the background.)

PAUL: *(To us, while he eats the biscuit:)* I'm not listening. I sit here, watching her, paying no attention to what she's saying. *(Beat)* Eating a biscuit. I'm the only one eating. *(Beat)* I've made a fool of myself. *(Beat)* At least I'm noticed. At least that. *(Eats)*

(Fade up on the room)

ADVICE TO EASTERN EUROPE

PETER: Paul? *(Beat)* Paul?!

PAUL: I'm sorry, I was just—

PETER: I was just saying that you spent some time at the *World Service*. Helena has a friend with the Czech service.

HELENA: A friend of my uncle's.

PAUL: I was with—.

PETER: Anyway, I was saying that the radio was totally different. The people at radio. As opposed to in television. At the B B C. Wouldn't you agree? *(Beat)* A whole different—.

HELENA: How are they different?

PAUL: I was only there for a summer. I was still in school. I was an intern. My father got me the job. He knew someone. He was with *Newsweek* then.

HELENA: You father then is a journalist?

PETER: *(Interrupting:)* In America they don't have radio. Did you know that?

PAUL: They have radio.

PETER: They don't listen.

HELENA: There's *Voice of America*. I have listened to Voice—.

PETER: In America they don't have *Voice of America*, isn't that right?

PAUL: That's—

PETER: Isn't that incredible. They don't have radio.

PAUL: They have—

PETER: They have music. Only music.

PAUL: They have talk shows.

PETER: There is no radio in America. The end! *(Short pause)* And it's a shame too. When a country gives up something like... Just turns it's back. You wonder what else, you know what I mean? There are hardly any railroads either.

PAUL: There's still—

PETER: They ripped them up. It's incredible when you go there.

HELENA: *(To* PAUL:*)* Have you been there?

PAUL: I'm American.

HELENA: I hadn't—. The accents I cannot hear—.

PETER: Not to be too critical, but the way I see it—they can't understand unless they see something now. They need pictures.

HELENA: In America.

PETER: What they see is what they believe. The rest, they just tune out. They have taught themselves to think in pictures. *(Beat)* That is why—when it comes to films—. Look at Steven Spielberg. He was something like twenty two when he made *Jaws*. Which grossed something like four hundred million. Take Lucas. They were kids thinking in pictures. You want to know what is wrong with the British film industry? People here are still listening! *(Beat)* We have radio. *(Beat)* But you finally have to ask yourself—is that wrong? Is this something we in England should hang our heads for?

(Fade out of conversation)

PAUL: *(To us:)* I don't know what Peter is talking about. *(Beat)* Sometimes he's like this after a drink or two.... Maybe it's her for him too. That beautiful face. *(He sighs.)* He's talking and even he isn't listening to himself. *(Laughs)*

(Fade in conversation)

PETER: Why is that funny, Paul?!

PAUL: I wasn't—

PETER: I spent sixteen years five months with the B B C. And maybe I didn't produce goddamn *Star Wars*, but I don't have many regrets. But Paul thinks it's just a joke.

PAUL: Peter, you don't—

PETER: Sometimes, Paul, I might agree with you. I might.

(Pause)

HELENA: They were very nice to me at White City. *(Beat)* They listened. We are going to talk again soon. *(Beat)* They told me a commercial producer would not be interested in such an idea for a film.

PETER: They always say that. And I'll bet you mentioned you were seeing me.

HELENA: Yes, I—.

(PETER *laughs.*)

(Short pause)

HELENA: But you are a distributor of films, no?

PETER: We plan to produce as well. That's why Paul's here. We're going to produce. He's reading scripts all the time, aren't you?

PAUL: Do you have a script?

(Fade out conversation)

PAUL: *(To us:)* So she writes screenplays? So she isn't a Czech film star? They have beautiful— Wait a minute —I didn't hear her answer.

(Fade in conversation)

PETER: I wouldn't believe a word they say at White City. They promise everyone everything. I could tell you stories…

(Fade out conversation)

PAUL: *(To us:)* Look at her. She thinks Peter's a fool. *(Beat)* And that's unfair. He's a very decent and accomplished man. I have learned a great deal from him. He has class. He really does. It's just sometimes—. He should know when to stop, is all. *(Beat)* Still, I hate it when people are quick to judge. Everyone feels that in a room when someone's doing that. It makes everyone uncomfortable. *(Beat)* Does she think this about me? Does she think that? *(Beat)* She sits there. She smokes. Every time I say something… *(Beat)* Also the minute I said I was an American. It was like that was that. She knew me. But how wrong can you be. If she knew me. *(Beat)* If only she knew. If only she—.

(Fade in conversation)

PETER: Paul? Paul?! Are you listening?

PAUL: What? Of course, I was just—

PETER: Then do you have the time?

PAUL: The—. It's—. I don't have a watch.

PETER: *(Laughing:)* He wasn't listening. *(Beat)* I have an appointment. I didn't know if you could take Helena to the club. As I have offered her a drink.

PAUL: To the—. If she—. Yeh.

PETER: Then you have the time?

PAUL: Uh…

HELENA: Perhaps his wife is waiting.

PAUL: No. She isn't. *(Beat)* She doesn't exist. I'm not married. I'm— *(Beat)* Anyone want this last biscuit? *(Begins to bite the biscuit and suddenly chokes.)*

HELENA: Are you all right?

PAUL: *(Choking:)* I'm—. I'm—

(Fade out)

2.

(A street in Soho)

PAUL: Dean Street's just to the left here. I'm sorry, you were saying...

HELENA: Please. I talk too much about myself.

PAUL: No, no, not at all—. I was just—.

HELENA: This is the bad of sudden, of so much change. And newness. I am getting very sick of my stories. *(She laughs.)*

PAUL: I doubt that. *(Beat)* For me that is very hard to—.

HELENA: I shall be very glad to be home and not have to tell a single story. This is true.

(PAUL laughs.)

PAUL: Except about London.

HELENA: Yes.

PAUL: New stories.

(Beat)

HELENA: Adventure stories, yes?

PAUL: Yes. *(Beat)* Whatever stories.

(Pause as HELENA and PAUL walk)

HELENA: Tell me about yourself. Why you are—as an American—.

PAUL: There's really nothing to—

HELENA: I doubt that! *(She laughs.)*

PAUL: Compared to you, I—

HELENA: Please.

PAUL: Well...

(Fade out. And fade into the memory of HELENA and PAUL being introduced in PETER's office, an hour or so earlier.)

(The office:)

HELENA: My name is Helena Lamicova. I was born November 14, 1963. In Prague. *(Beat)* For most of my life I have been in the motion pictures. First as editor working for my father who has made many well-known Czech films. Even two after sixty eight. I've met your father—. And more recently I work with my father as his co-screenwriter. It was he who sent me to London to see now that there is freedom and democracy in my country what projects the West might be interested in. *(Beat)* We have many ideas. *(Beat)* We have many talented artists ready to work. *(Beat)* I wish to take your time please and talk about some ideas.

PETER: Let me get Paul, he's my development person, *(Into a phone:)* Paul, do you have a second please? *(Beat)* He's coming.

HELENA: Then I will wait.

(Short pause)

PETER: Tea? *(Rustles with the kettle)* I'll have to fill it.

HELENA: Do not bother for—.

PETER: I'll get Paul to—. I have admired your father's work for years, of course. An extraordinary director. *(Beat)* One of the greats.

HELENA: He is not well.

PETER: I'm sorry to hear that.

(Short pause)

HELENA: To have waited for such a long time. A lifetime, and now—. When there is no one to stop you. *(Beat)* He tries to get out of bed. And then he is in pain for a week.

(PAUL enters.)

PAUL: I'm sorry, I didn't know you had—

ADVICE TO EASTERN EUROPE

PETER: Come in, come in. Paul, let me introduce you to—

(Fade out, fade back up on the street in SoHo. PAUL *is talking about himself:)*

PAUL: Finally I had to say to myself: I don't like American movies—by and large. There's the odd exception of course. I enjoy foreign films. Like your father's for example. There's just so much more— meat, is the word.. And the rhythm—it's not like life is always racing away. The world is not one big car chase with music playing furiously underneath. It's not real. *(Beat)* I guess—that is part of their point, isn't it — to not be real. Anyway, the scripts for American movies—.

HELENA: Yes.

PAUL: As a screenwriter yourself, they must make you—

HELENA: I do not criticize other writers.

PAUL: Ah.

(HELENA *and* PAUL *walk.)*

PAUL: That's noble. *(Beat)* Still—so I didn't like the films. I didn't like the T V. Again, by and large. Again, there's the exception. I didn't like the way the politicians were acting. Everything about American politics right now.... You either laugh or cry, if you know what I mean. And then there was a whole lot of other shit. Personal problems. Girlfriend problems. *(Beat)* Everything. *(Beat)* So when my Mother died—. I said, why not? She was Canadian. So I got a dual passport. And… They let Canadians work here. Though I've only myself been to Canada once in my life and that was to the other side of Niagara Falls. *(He laughs.)* No, once I went to Toronto. For a film festival, *(Beat)* I forgot about that. *(Beat)* So twice. *(He laughs.)*

(Pause)

HELENA: Then you must like British movies then.

PAUL: What British movies? *(He laughs.)* It's right here.

(PAUL *opens a door and* HELENA *and* PAUL *go in, street noise now in the distance.)*

PAUL: We have to sign in. I do. Give them my number.

RECEPTIONIST: Are you the member?

PAUL: Yes. Yes I am.

RECEPTIONIST: You're signing in the wrong space, The member signs there.

PAUL: Right. *(He signs.)* I don't come here that often.

HELENA: It's nice.

PAUL: It's okay.

(*As* HELENA *and* PAUL *go into the bar:)*

PAUL: There... There's two seats there. Let's grab them. Hurry. *(He hurries off.)* They're taken. There's a jacket. *(He looks around.)* You must have clubs like this in Prague. There's two!

(HELENA *and* PAUL *go to their seats.)*

PAUL: How's this?

HELENA: Very pleasant.

PAUL: It is, isn't it. Now let's see if we can find a waitress. *(Beat)* You must have clubs like this in Prague. Or have I already asked you that?

HELENA: We have one or two.

PAUL: When I visit you, you must take me.

HELENA: You will be visiting Prague?

PAUL: There's a waitress. What do you want? White wine?

HELENA: Wine would be fine.

ADVICE TO EASTERN EUROPE

PAUL: The wine's good here. *(Calls:)* Waitress! *(Beat)* She's coming. *(Beat)* If we are working on a film together, I will have to go to Prague, won't I?

HELENA: We are working—?

PAUL: Who knows. *(Beat)* I thought she saw us. *(Beat)* You don't have to pay money here. It all goes on a bill.

HELENA: I see. This is convenient.

PAUL: I'd love to go to Prague just to meet your father.

HELENA: He'd be honored.

PAUL: I think he's one of the four or five great film makers of all time. I mean, I rate him with John Ford, of course. Renoir. Fassbinder.

HELENA: I do not like Fassbinder.

PAUL: On that I am prepared to argue all day. *(He laughs.)* Here she is. It was a white wine, right?

(Fade the sounds of the club into the distance.)

PAUL: *(To us:)* I'm going to ask her to dinner. She's said nothing about what she was doing tonight. And I've given her a million chances. *(Beat)* I think she wants me to ask her to dinner tonight. *(Beat)* I'll call my friend, Henry, tell him I can't explain American football tonight to him, which is what he's been wanting me to do for decades, and I will take her out to dinner. *(Beat)* I'll say the company would want it. *(Beat)* After all, we're practically working together, aren't we? *(Beat)* On the company, I'll say. *(Short pause)* Or maybe we'll see a movie. I'll get *Time Out*. They must have it somewhere here. A place like this. Someone must have a copy. *(Beat)* A movie. That's business. *(Beat)* Something we can talk about together then. After. At dinner.

(Fade in the club; HELENA *in the middle of a talk.)*

HELENA: There are three ideas. That we have come up with. My father and I have tried to see things from a Westerner's perspective. We're interested in making movies that will work just as well in the West.

PAUL: Yes. This is essential. *(Beat)* But without of course lowering—..

HELENA: I do not thing that is a question.

PAUL: Just so—. Well, there's a feeling, that feeling your father is able to convey—. It's a texture. By Western—by American standards it would be slow, but—. I wouldn't want to see him lose—.

HELENA: If he has the right subject.

PAUL: Yes. *(Beat)* This is true. I shouldn't be worrying.

HELENA: And there are the three that I have mentioned. *(Beat)* But I only wish to tell you about one.

PAUL: Tell me whatever one you want to tell me.

HELENA: It is the one that the B B C has expressed so much interest in.

PAUL: Right. But they haven't bought—.

HELENA: No. *(Beat)* Not yet. *(She sips her wine.)* It needs only to be approved by—. The one who approves. And then there will be a commission?

PAUL: I suppose so. It can work that way. *(Beat)* It can work other ways.

HELENA: They were very excited. It is the most interesting.

PAUL: We could also co-commission with the B B C. We're not exactly in competition. We could do the feature. Something can always be worked out. *(Beat)* In fact, I happen to know that they're looking for this sort of arrangements right now.

HELENA: Are they?

PAUL: It fits in.

HELENA: Good.

(Short pause)

PAUL: Another wine?

HELENA: Are you having—?

PAUL: Absolutely. Two then. I'll get her attention. *(Beat)* It's good isn't it? The wine.

HELENA: Very good.

(Short pause)

PAUL: As soon as she turns around. *(Beat)* I'm not keeping you from anywhere, am I?

HELENA: No. *(Beat)* Not at all. *(Beat)* I have no where to go.

PAUL: *(Calls:)* The same please! Thank you. *(Beat)* She'll bring them.

HELENA: So, should I...?

PAUL: Please. I'm all ears.

(Beat)

HELENA: So. You have read I am sure the play by Chekhov, *Three Sisters*?

PAUL: I'm sure I have. *Three Sisters*. I think in college. I must have. Sure.

HELENA: Well, the idea is this. We follow the three sisters, Olga, Masha, Irina, after they leave their home in the provinces, years after the play ends, after the Russian revolution in fact, but instead of going to Moscow as they say they will in the play, do you know where they go to?

PAUL: No. *(Beat)* Where?

HELENA: New York City. *(Beat)* New York City. America. *(Beat)* Interesting, isn't it? New York. This is the location for the film.

PAUL: Does your father know New York—.

HELENA: My father is ill. He will supervise the film, of course. But whether he is well enough to direct. This is not the only reason you are—

PAUL: No, of course not. So far it sounds great.

HELENA: It is this location of New York that will make the story—I don't know. Not so…

PAUL: Foreign?

HELENA: I suppose, yes. This is what my father says. *(Beat)* Westerners need to see places they know. This is one thing that very much attracts an audience. Is that right?

PAUL: I— *(Beat)* Huh. I hadn't thought of it that way.

HELENA: Also, and I was against this at first, but my father insisted. We do the film in English.

PAUL: That's a very good idea.

HELENA: I would need a writer to work with me. My English… Though perhaps the actors would help too.

PAUL: I think they usually do.

HELENA: I thought perhaps of Meryl Streep? This is a good idea for one of the sisters?

PAUL: You could do worse.

HELENA: A very—commercial idea, no?

PAUL: And she's an excellent actress.

HELENA: She's a very big star in Czechoslovakia. People adore her. I don't know if this matters, but she would sell many many tickets in Czechoslovakia,

PAUL: Every ticket counts.

(Fade out the club)

3.

(The Club)

(Fade up. HELENA *and* PAUL *talking with* GERALD. *A little while later)*

GERALD: I've been to—let me think. This year, Bucharest. Moscow. I almost went to Prague.

HELENA: When you do come...

GERALD: I'll need to get your address.

(Short pause)

PAUL: Gerald is working on a screenplay for us.

HELENA: I see. You're a writer, but I thought you taught—.

GERALD: Mostly I teach. I'd even go so far as to say I see myself mostly as a teacher now. And I'm not ashamed to say that. I gladly leave the literary rat race to the hungry kids, like Paul.

PAUL: Thank you.

GERALD: Though still, every now and then, I still get the idea that just might titilate the masses. *(He laughs.)* And I'm not ashamed of that either.

PAUL: He's not ashamed of much.

GERALD: I'm hard to shame. *(Laughs)*

(Pause)

PAUL: Gerald has written a number of screenplays.

GERALD: *(To* HELENA, *ignoring* PAUL:*)* You should come to Cambridge. It's very beautiful.

HELENA: You will give me your address then.

PAUL: How long have you been teaching at Cambridge, Gerald? I thought it was a one-year sort of thing.

GERALD: *(Ignoring him:)* I have extraordinary rooms. And the most incredible dinner conversations in commons. Scientists. Scholars. Politicians.

PAUL: Gerald's screenplay for us is about Jack The Ripper.

HELENA: Really?

GERALD: A grotesque.

PAUL: A sort of *Friday The 13th Part Twenty-Seven* set in London—for kids. To scare kids on dates. That sort of movie.

GERALD: I love Agatha Christie. I find that it's the best way to get to sleep. After a hard day. *(Beat)* One of the two best ways to get to sleep. *(He laughs.)*

(HELENA *laughs.*)

GERALD: Let me get us another drink.

PAUL: I think we're—

GERALD: You've got this on the company, don't you, Paul? After all, we've brought up my film, it's already like a story conference. *(Calls:)* The same, please!

HELENA: Why were you in Moscow?

GERALD: With the festival? The Moscow—.

HELENA: Film festival?

PAUL: He—

GERALD: I was—how do you say it—a...

HELENA: Judge?

GERALD: That's right.

HELENA: You were a judge this year at the Moscow—.

ADVICE TO EASTERN EUROPE

PAUL: They wanted a commercial voice. An American commercial voice. Gerald is American, by the way. You'd never know though by the accent.

GERALD: Do I have an accent? Really? I guess when you're in one place as long as—.

PAUL: And you voted for—. At the...festival. He told me this, he was proud of it — said, how did you put it, it was time to kick a little cultural ass? So you voted to give the golden palm or the shining hammer and sickle to whatever was the closest equivalent to *Friday The 13th Part Twenty-Seven* there was.

GERALD: The piece was very Orwellian. And I mean Orson Wellian. *(Laughs)* Also very Polanski.

PAUL: You said it was shlock, Gerald.

GERALD: I think when one accepts such a position—as I did with quite a bit of hesitancy—.

PAUL: About three seconds.

GERALD: You have the responsibility to shake things up. *(Beat)* If they'd wanted someone who was going to agree.... Cheer on the usual foreign piece of obscurity. I told them, they should have got Jarmusch or Greenaway. Or some German. *(Beat)* What made me finally decide to accept was the realization that for them—over there, with all they are going through, trying to be the way they think we are, I suppose. *(Laughs)* Is that right?

HELENA: I don't know.

GERALD: Anyway, I realized that the mainstream—the shlock is now their avant-garde. In the East. So I was in fact the only true voice of this future. Of the way things are headed. *(Beat)* And in this way I was listened to. *(Beat)* And my opinions and advice sought out. *(Beat)* I was pleased I went. I felt I hadn't wasted my time.

(Pause)

HELENA: I forget, what won the Moscow Film Festival this year?

(Short pause)

PAUL: Television. This was the Moscow Television Festival.

HELENA: I've never heard—

GERALD: It's very prestigious. There are a lot of buyers.

PAUL: It's run by a Swiss distributor and held at the auditorium of the Swiss Embassy.

GERALD: It's a beautiful auditorium. Large. But not too large. *(Pause)* In my three days in Moscow, you could feel the change in the air. Everywhere. Like the shackles had been suddenly lifted off. *(Beat)* History was in the air. *(Beat)* I felt like I should have had a camera with me. Doing a documentary. Recording—

PAUL: I think it is being recorded.

(Pause)

GERALD: Are you two going to talk business or can I—?

PAUL: Please. Sit down and join us.

(Short pause)

GERALD: I didn't catch your name?

HELENA: Helena.

GERALD: Gerald.

HELENA: How do you do.

(Pause)

GERALD: How long are you here for?

HELENA: I go back tomorrow morning.

GERALD: Short visit.

HELENA: I have been here two weeks.

GERALD: That's not so short. *(Short pause)* If you're not doing anything tonight, I have—. I was thinking of going out to dinner. There's a restaurant—. They know me. It's not easy to get—

PAUL: Helena has—.

HELENA: Paul and I are having dinner. Isn't that right?

PAUL: Yes. *(Beat)* That is right.

GERALD: I see. I wouldn't want to—.

PAUL: And we might see something. If that's all—.

HELENA: I'd love to.

PAUL: I was looking for a *Time Out* to see what there was. You don't happen to have this week's *Time Out*, do you, Gerald?

GERALD: In my briefcase. *(Beat)* Over there. *(Beat)* I'll get it. *(He gets up and goes.)*

(Short pause)

PAUL: We'll see what's on.

HELENA: Very good.

PAUL: There's lots of things.

HELENA: I'm sure.

(Beat)

PAUL: Have you seen anything?

HELENA: No. *(Beat)* A few films. Some television in my hotel room. *(Beat)* In the television room at my hotel. In the sitting room.

(Short pause)

PAUL: We'll see something then. *(Beat)* You can't go back to Prague without soaking up some British culture.

(Fade out)

4.

(Opera House, Covent Garden)

(During a performance of Janáček's Kát'a Kabanová.)

(Act Three, Kata's aria, is heard for a while.)

(Fade the opera into the distance.)

PAUL: *(To us:)* An opera. *(Beat)* Sung in Czech. *(Beat)* I was surprised. I'd thought—. What I'd been suggesting—. With her being here. When I go to another country, I like to see things which— Well, I certainly do not want to see say an American movie when I'm say in Greece. *(Laughs)* I don't understand that. The whole point—or at least some of the point of going to a foreign place is you give up—for a while—your—. What? Home? Things you know. What you are easy with? *(Beat)* Anyway. *(Laughs to himself)* Kát'a Kabanová. By Leoš Janáček.

(Fade back in the opera for a short while.)

(Fade the opera back into the distance.)

PAUL: *(To us:)* I suggested, after we finally got the *Timeout* out of Gerald—and that took two or three reminders by the way—I suggested—. There are a number of films. I thought maybe if we saw a film together, you know. Makes sense. *(Beat)* A film for Christ sake. *(Beat)* If we are going to be working together. *(Beat)* Her idea about *Three Sisters*, I think, is actually quite interesting. There's a lot of promise there. Combines many many things.

(Short pause)

(PAUL unwraps a mint. Someone near "sh-shs" him.)

PAUL: Well, there just wasn't a film—. That she wanted to see. Half of them I don't think she'd ever heard of—how could she have—so how she knew she didn't want to see them... *(Beat)* She said no to a play. She said no to a musical. That could have been a lark. I hate musicals myself. They're very—obvious. They're an element of America I really dislike. It's like when the English say about an American musical that it has a lot of innocence and a lot of energy. *(Beat)* I cringe. *(Beat)* Still I would have gone with Helena for a laugh. *(Beat)* As we walked through Soho with Gerald's *Time Out*, which he sold me—and this on a Tuesday and the new one is coming out what? Tomorrow? I said—

(Fade out opera house, fade in Soho street.)

PAUL: It'll be silly. But it could be fun. As long as you don't think this is the sort of thing I go to see all the time. I haven't been to a musical in—.

HELENA: I do like music. *(Beat)* I love the opera.

PAUL: Maybe there's an opera—.

HELENA: I saw a poster back there in the front of a shop. Do you know *Kát'a Kabanová*?

PAUL: Is she a—?

HELENA: By Janáček? It's at the Opera House?

(Short pause)

PAUL: If that's what you'd like—.

HELENA: If you haven't seen it. I'd only go so you could see—.

PAUL: If it's what you want to do. I live here.

HELENA: Maybe we should see a film. You want to see a film.

PAUL: An opera's fine. Please. Though I doubt if we can get tickets.

HELENA: We can walk in that direction. Which direction?

PAUL: And if we can't get in, we'll see a—.

(Fade out street, fade in more of Kát'a.*)*

(Fade opera into background.)

PAUL: *(To us:)* I don't know what's going on in this. I don't know this opera. *(Beat)* It's in Czech. *(Beat)* It's interesting. *(Beat)* At first that's why I thought—. Because it's Czech, why Helena wanted—. I thought perhaps it hadn't been allowed to be performed for—. Whatever. So… *(Beat)* But it turned out she'd seen it twenty times. In Prague. *(Beat)* She wanted me to see it. I am enjoying it. *(Beat)* The fact that your mind wanders a little does not imply you are not enjoying—.

(Fade out of opera house, fade up street in front of the opera house.)

PAUL: *(Approaching* HELENA:*)* I got two—together. They're at the side.

HELENA: That's wonderful.

PAUL: I don't think they're great seats.

HELENA: Thank you. I can't wait to see your reaction; you will—.

(Fade conversation)

PAUL: *(To us:)* She took my hand and held it.

(Fade back to street)

HELENA: We have an hour, what do you want to do?

PAUL: There's a pub I know…

HELENA: That would be nice.

PAUL: I think I remember which one. It's quite famous. Let me think…

HELENA: A pub. *(Beat)* Or a bookshop? Do you like to browse in bookshops?

PAUL: Uh. Sure. Yeh. If you want to go to a bookshop.

HELENA: No, a pub's fine.

ADVICE TO EASTERN EUROPE

PAUL: There's a bookshop just—.

HELENA: Paul, you want to go to a pub.

(Fade out street, fade in bookshop.)

HELENA: *(To* CLERK:*)* Excuse me.

CLERK: Yes?

HELENA: Is there a section for Czech writers?

CLERK: I'm sorry, all fiction writers are together. All poets—

HELENA: I see, thank you.

PAUL: *(To us:)* She was only interested, at least at first, in seeing which Czech writers were published in the West. How their books looked. The jacket designs.... *(Beat)* I picked up a Milan Kundera...

HELENA: He is not nearly so respected now.

PAUL: Kundera? But he's one of the greatest novelists—.

(Fade bookshop into distance)

PAUL: *(To us:)* But she was off. *(Beat)* I watched her reach under a table. She bends down. Then reached. *(Beat)* She's beautiful. Her legs and knees. Her skirt just above the knee.

(Fade in bookshop)

HELENA: Here. This we should get and talk about at dinner. *(Beat)* It's *Three Sisters*. *(Beat)* Is it a good translation? There seems to be many translations. *(She reads:)* "The music Is happy and alive, and It seems that some time soon we will know why we live, why we—."

PAUL: *(To us:)* For no reason, or so It seemed, she reached over and hugged me against my shoulder. *(Beat)* I kissed her on the cheek. *(He kisses her.)* There In Dillons. Downstairs. On Southampton Street. *(Beat)*

The shop that had been the old Arts Council Bookshop. *(Beat)* What Thatcher did to the Arts Council. *(Beat)* But if she hadn't…. It would not now be Dillons and would not have been open this late, and Helena and I would not be here In it's basement. By the plays. The classical plays. *(Short pause)* On her left cheek. *(Beat)* And she closed her eyes.

(Suddenly the soaring of Kát'a at the opera house. the moment where Kát'a sings: "You are my life, my joy, my soul—and how I love you!" —In Czech.)

(After a moment:)

PAUL: *(Whispers to* HELENA:*)* I love it.

HELENA: What?

PAUL: I love—it.

(Music continues until)

5.

(A restaurant)

HELENA: *(Reading from the end of* Three Sisters:*)* "Listen—the music!" Masha says. "They're leaving us, one has left forever and ever, we're left alone to start again. We must keep living… We must keep living…" *(Beat)* Irina now puts her head on Olga's breast. "The time will come when everyone will know the reason for this suffering and there will be no more mysteries. We must keep living… We must work, just work! Tomorrow I'll go away alone, I'll teach and devote the rest of my life to others who may need it. It's Fall now, then Winter and the snow will cover over everything, and I shall work, just work… *(She sips her wine.)*

PAUL: Let me pour some more. *(He pours.)*

*(*HELENA *continues to read:)*

HELENA: Olga now embraces both of her sisters: "The way the band is playing, it sounds so happy, so brave, you do want to keep living. My God, time will go by and we will be dead forever; they will forget our faces, voices, even how many we were, but upon our suffering, their joy will be built, happiness and peace will rule the world, and we who live today will be spoken kindly of and thanked. Dear sister, our lives aren't over yet. Let us live. The music is happy and alive, and it seems that some time soon we will know why we live, why we suffer... If only we knew. If only we knew." *(Beat. She closes the book. Pause)* And this is how we begin. In my story. *(Beat)* You have this—it's a longing to know. To change. To begin again. *(Beat)* The revolution is to come soon. *(Beat)* We change the date of the story so they are not too old. But you can see that they will escape. The three of them. *(Beat)* It's what they're saying. *(Beat)* First through Eastern Europe. Where there is the war. *(Beat)* Then south to the Mediterranean. And onto a boat. *(Beat)* We can show this. We cannot show this. This depends upon the budget for the film.

PAUL: I don't think we should limit ourselves yet, before—

HELENA: We should be realistic. *(Beat)* I do not want people to read the screenplay and say this is very nice, very exciting story but too expensive, sorry. No, we must not let this happen. *(Beat)* So we either show this or we put it on a title and do it that way. Anway, the story is when the three sisters arrive in New York City.

(Short pause)

PAUL: You're not eating.

HELENA: I shall eat. *(She takes a bite.)* My father and I have talked about this story for years. We could write it in no more than days. We have thought it all out.

(Beat) We would write in Czech. We should need a writer who writes in English.

PAUL: I know one or two.

HELENA: A good one. Who understands—.

PAUL: I know one or two.

(Short pause)

HELENA: I'm sure you must. *(Short pause)* Obviously they end up in the Russian ghetto in New York City. This in in Manhattan, is it not?

PAUL: I think—. It was. Also, the—. They're not Jewish?

HELENA: No. Definitely not. *(Beat)* They see America as their hope. As they land upon the shore, they are overtaken by the bigness of America.

PAUL: The skyscrapers—

HELENA: And of the people who are busy and, one will say to the other—full of purpose. *(Beat)* And there is bread on the shelves in the shops. There is work. Irina will become the teacher she wishes to become. She is allowed now to become what she could not before be. *(Beat)* Of course, bad things do happen. Olga will die from disease. Masha will marry again, but again not happily. So not everything is changed.

We cannot change who we are, even in a new place, This is the idea. *(Beat)* If we are bad people living in a hell, we will also be a bad people living in a heaven.

PAUL: Heaven? I think—

HELENA: But to know that there is a hell and a heaven, this gives one hope, this—

PAUL: I think— *(Stops himself)*

HELENA: What?

(Beat)

PAUL: Well, I think you're idealizing... *(Beat)* Wouldn't a more intersting story—one closer to reality as well—be something like, I don't know, the sisters arrive in New York and after some time realize that, well, that there are problems here as well.

HELENA: Of course there will be problems, They shall face all these problems.

PAUL: I don't mean, someone getting sick. Actually, I think—as an American—that the country is living one great big lie. I'm not saying it always was, but—. I just don't think even you'd like it, let alone you're three sisters.

HELENA: They are escaping. They have no where else to go.

PAUL: I understand this.

HELENA: It is safe. There is peace. There is a chance to do what one wishes—.

PAUL: Not really. That's not really true, if you—

HELENA: You say you can't do what you want?!

PAUL: Depends upon who you are. What your education is. How much money—

HELENA: You say you can't walk into a shop and buy what you wish?

PAUL: If you have the money to—

HELENA: You can say things. You are not arrested.

PAUL: Were your sisters going to be arrested if—.

HELENA: They might have! They didn't know! No one knew! It was chaos! You don't know what it was like.

PAUL: In America in 1917, they might have found some work, but within fifteen years, the odds were hat they'd be out in the street without—.

HELENA: Not if they worked, Paul!

PAUL: You sound like you come from goddamn Arizona, not Czechoslovakia!! I don't believe we're having this argument. Look, I won't say America is all bad—.

HELENA: I do not say it is all good.

PAUL: Thank you. *(Beat)* Thank you.

HELENA: But when you compare—.

PAUL: That's right, when you have compared, then I still want you to say—.

HELENA: You don't let me finish my thinking!

(Pause)

PAUL: Finish.

(Short pause)

HELENA: If you work, you make money. With money you can buy things, because there are things to buy. *(Beat)* This is America. *(Beat)* This is the West. This is England too. *(Short pause)* I know you do not live there now. So you must criticize.

PAUL: That's not the reason—.

HELENA: You must have your excuse for what you do. But what you do, Paul, it is like leaving your family. Getting away from one's Mother and Father. For a while. *(Beat)* It is a part of adolescence. You leave to grow up. You do not leave to survive. You keep your passport, I am sure.

PAUL: Of course, I—.

HELENA: You will go back. This—here—in England is your "fling". That is a word?

PAUL: Yes, that's—

HELENA: So you must criticize. You must grow up.

PAUL: I'm twenty seven. I think I've grown up!

(HELENA *laughs.*)

PAUL: You're no older, Helena.

HELENA: In years, I am not. No. *(Beat)* No, not in years, Paul.

(Long pause)

(HELENA *and* PAUL *eat.*)

HELENA: I will pay for my own dinner, please. I have decided this.

PAUL: I told you the company will pay. *(Pause)* It's business, isn't it? *(Beat)* That is what it is. *(Short pause)* So the three sisters come to the United States and find heaven on earth. *(He laughs to himself.)* That's your story. That's what you want to sell. *(He laughs again.)*

HELENA: They find a place where human relations can grow at their own pace—without the world encroaching.

PAUL: As if the world were one thing and their human relations were another.

HELENA: They often are.

PAUL: *(To himself:)* I do not believe I'm hearing this!

HELENA: You would want this. If you had experienced—

PAUL: I have experienced! I am not a goddamn child to be told how wonderful a childhood I have had!! *(Short pause)* Sorry. *(Long pause)* I have long considered your father one of the great film directors in the world. It would be a great pleasure to meet him. Let alone work with him....

(Pause)

HELENA: *(Eating:)* Come to Prague.

PAUL: *(Eating:)* Which I understand is very beautiful. Very—attractive. *(Short pause)* The opera was very enjoyable. *(Beat)* Thank you for suggesting it.

HELENA: I have heard it sung much better. *(Short pause)* I shall need to get back to my hotel very soon.

PAUL: You don't want coffee, do you?*(Long pause)* Look, I'm sorry. You just touched on something—. It's—. Right now in the States, probably the most irritating thing is the way so many Americans look at what's been happening in the world. With your country. With Romania. With—everything. And they delude themselves to think that—and they will even say this: well, we've won! *(Laughs)* It's true! They have misunderstood by that much. *(Beat)* They say, and I have heard them say this—that what it's all been about, is how everyone—everyone wants to be like them. Like America. *(Beat)* So when you have that kind of madness—. What you said, it touched this—. I'm frustrated because there is no one really saying, this is not true fellas. You don't get it, do you? You have completely missed the point about what is happening.

(Short pause)

HELENA: Why isn't it, true?

PAUL: What do you mean?

HELENA: You say they delude themselves to think—

PAUL: Yeh.

HELENA: But I don't think they are deluding themselves, Paul. People do want to be like America.

PAUL: Then they don't understand—.

HELENA: They see what you have and—

PAUL: They don't see!

HELENA: For years we have heard there is so much crime, so much selfishness, there are the racists! But who told us this? The same people who told us lie after lie after lie!!

PAUL: *(Shouting:)* You don't understand, understand!!!! You don't.

(Short pause)

WAITER: Quiet, please. You are disturbing other people, Please be a little quieter.

(Fade out the restaurant)

6.

(Drury Lane)

*(*PAUL *following* HELENA *who is walking fast.)*

PAUL: The Strand's the best place. You get them coming across Waterloo—

HELENA: There's a taxi there!

PAUL: You won't get it.

HELENA: *(Calling and running:)* Taxi! Taxi!

PAUL: *(To us:)* She won't get it. *(Beat)* Watch the puddle, Helena. Watch the… *(He laughs to himself.)* Puddle. She stepped right in it.

*(*HELENA *approaches.)*

HELENA: He didn't see me.

PAUL: I don't think his light was even on. *(Short pause)* The best place is the Strand.

HELENA: Do you have something I can clean my legs with?

PAUL: I saw you step in—

HELENA: A tissue? A handkerchief. Look at the mud.

(Short pause)

PAUL: I have a handkerchief. *(Beat)* Here.

HELENA: Could you hold my arm, so I can—.

(Beat)

(PAUL *holds* HELENA's *arm.*)

HELENA: Thank you. *(Beat)* I should not have worn stockings. Look at this Any more mud on the back of my leg?

PAUL: No. *(Beat)* I don't see… *(Beat)* A little spot.

HELENA: Could you…? *(Beat)* Thank you. *(Short pause)* We should go to the Strand.

PAUL: What are you doing?

HELENA: Your shirt was untucked, Paul, I was tucking in your shirt.

(Fade out Drury Lane)

7.

(Street near Russell Square)

(Thunder, and a downpour)

(HELENA *and* PAUL *running.*)

HELENA: *(Laughing:)* We're soaked.

PAUL: Keep your-program over your head.

HELENA: It's falling apart!

(HELENA *and* PAUL *both laugh.*)

HELENA: We're almost there.

(HELENA *and* PAUL *hurry.*)

HELENA: We should have taken the taxi.

PAUL: We should have found someplace to sit and wait. It doesn't rain like this—.

HELENA: I need to get back to the hotel, Paul.

PAUL: Watch it!

(HELENA *and* PAUL *are splashed by a car.*)

PAUL: *(To the car:)* Hey, come on!!

HELENA: It doesn't matter. My shoes are already full of water.

(Thunder)

PAUL: It's getting worse. Run. *(Beat)* Come on, run, Helena! Take off your shoes! Here give me your shoes!

(HELENA *and* PAUL *run. Fade out street*)

8.

(HELENA'*s room in her bed and breakfast.*)

PAUL: You don't think they'll mind? *(Beat)* The couple downstairs. The man saw us come up.

HELENA: Why should they care. You are my guest.

PAUL: Some of these places—

HELENA: I am sorry I cannot offer a robe. I have only this one robe.

(Beat)

PAUL: Why should you bring two robes? *(He laughs.)* My pants will be dry soon. The heater is on now.

(Short pause)

HELENA: The shower felt… *(Beat)* A warm shower? You don't want to take a shower? *(Beat)* I paid extra to have this shower.

(Pause)

PAUL: Does the radio work?

HELENA: I haven't—

PAUL: *(At the radio:)* Sometimes they read a book—. On radio, they...

(PAUL *tunes the radio.)*

PAUL: Here.

(Throughout the remainder of the scene, chapter 16 of A Room With A View *is read.)*

RADIO: "But Lucy had developed since the spring. That is to say, she was now better able to stifle the emotions of which the conventions and the world disapprove. Though the danger was greater, she was not shaken by deep sobs."

HELENA: What is it?

PAUL: I don't know. Should I turn it off?

HELENA: It's nice.

RADIO: *(Continuing:)* "She said to Cecil, 'I am not coming in to tea—tell mother—I must write some letter,' and went up to her room. Then she prepared for action. She felt and returned, love which is the most real thing that we shall ever meet, reappeared—."

HELENA: You're cold, Paul. Please. Put the blanket around you.

RADIO: "—now as the world's enemy, and she must stifle it. She sent for Miss Bartlett."

PAUL: I'm fine.

RADIO: "The contest lay not between love and duty. Perhaps there never is such a contest. It lay between the real—."

HELENA: You're shivering. *(Beat)* Come on, at least get under the blankets if you're going to sit there.

PAUL: I don't have to sit—.

HELENA: Please.

PAUL: I'm getting under the blankets.

RADIO: "—and the pretended, and Lucy's first aim was to defeat herself. As her brain clouded over, as the memory of the views grew dim and the words of the book died away, she returned to her old shibboleth of nerves. She 'conquered her breakdown.' Tampering with the truth, she forgot that the truth had ever been. Remembering that she was engaged to Cecil, she—."

PAUL: Aren't you warm in that robe?

HELENA: Now that you mention it. *(Beat)* I am. *(Beat)* I better take it off.

RADIO: "—compelled herself to confused remembrances of George; he was nothing to her; he never had been anything; he had behaved abominably—."

(Squeaks of bedsprings)

PAUL: Do you want the radio off?

HELENA: It's funny. I like it.

RADIO: "—she had never encouraged him. The armour of falsehood is subtly wrought out of darkness, and hides a man not only from others—."

(Bedsprings)

RADIO: "—but from his own soul. In a few moments Lucy—"

9.

(Holborn Tube Station. Morning)

PAUL: The flight's in an hour and a half? You'll make it. The tube usually takes about fifty minutes. *(Beat)* There. There's one coming in two minutes.

(Pause)

HELENA: I can take my bag now.

(Short pause)

PAUL: That lady, when she saw me come down the stairs with you. *(He laughs.)*

HELENA: What?

PAUL: Her face.

HELENA: I don't think she cares. *(Beat)* It can't be something new to her. She runs a hotel after all.

(Beat)

PAUL: I suppose, yeh.

(Pause)

HELENA: Thank you.

PAUL: For what?

HELENA: So I shall see you in Prague next?

PAUL: Absolutely. Or here. Maybe we'll get you back here. Whatever Peter says. *(Short pause)* I'd love to come to Prague.

HELENA: To meet my father. *(Beat)* To work with us on the film.

(Beat)

PAUL: For many reasons. *(Short pause)* To argue politics with you. *(He smiles.)* I will miss this.

HELENA: This is what you'll miss? *(She laughs.)* You come to Prague and say how great you think socialism is, I shall not be able to show you to my friends.

PAUL: We shall see what happens.

HELENA: Yes.

PAUL: You'll learn. You'll see.

HELENA: Maybe.

(Beat)

ADVICE TO EASTERN EUROPE

PAUL: I will convince you! *(He laughs.)*

HELENA: Paul, please!

PAUL: What? I don't—

HELENA: I think—. Maybe we should not talk politics for a time. You have a lifetime of it and you must understand, I wish it all just to go away.

PAUL: I was just teasing—.

HELENA: I know. *(Beat)* I know you were. The train will be here...

PAUL: The opera was terrific.

HELENA: And the book on the radio.

PAUL: A great story.

(Beat)

HELENA: Paul... *(She kisses him.)* You know, I have fallen in love with you.

(Train pulls in.)

HELENA: Here. You take this. And study it!

PAUL: What is—?!

HELENA: Goodbye!

PAUL: I'll call when Peter's made a decision!

HELENA: We shall see what happens! Goodbye!!!!

(Train closes its doors and pulls out.)

PAUL: *(To himself:)* See you soon. *(Beat)* Please.

(Pause)

(Fade tube station into the distance)

PAUL: *(To us:)* She had handed me the copy of Chekhov's *Three Sisters* she'd bought last night at Dillons and had read from at dinner. *(Beat)* The last page was marked. This was what I was to study. I opened it while going up the escalator at the Holborn

Station. I decided to walk to Wardour Street. *(Short pause. He reads:)* "My God, time will go by and we will be dead forever; they will forget our faces, voices, even how many we were, but upon our suffering, their joy will be built, happiness and peace will rule the world, and we who live today will be spoken kindly of and thanked. Dear sisters our lives aren't over yet. Let us live. The music is happy and alive, and it seems that sometime soon we will know why we live, why we suffer... If only we knew. If only we knew."

(The street. PAUL *walks through a crowd.)*

PAUL: *(To us:)* We shall see what happens.

(Pause)

END OF PLAY

THE AMERICAN WIFE

THE AMERICAN WIFE was first broadcast on B B C Radio 4 on 24 November 1994. The cast was as follows:

ANN DAY	Zoë Wanamaker
HARRY DAY	Anton Lesser
FIONA	Emily Richard
JOHN	Oliver Cotton
SAM BEACH	John Sharian
SETH	Alan Harriot
GIRLFRIEND	Gona Beeson
MOTHER	Melinda
Director	Ned Chaillet

CHARACTERS & SETTING

ANN DAY, *thirties, American.*
HARRY DAY, *forties, English. A film producer.*
FIONA, *forties, English, an editor in a book publishing house.*
JOHN, FIONA's *husband, fifties, English.*
SAM BEACH, *twenties, American, novelist.*

The play takes place on Thanksgiving day (the third Thursday of November) in the home of ANN *and* HARRY DAY, *Hammersmith, London.*

for Zoë Wanamaker

(A house in Hammersmith, London)

(A November afternoon)

(ANN, an American woman in her twenties, speaks to us.)

ANN: *(To us:)* There's the theatre. The parks. It's pretty safe. Harry's English. *(Beat)* So now I've been in England for three years. At first it was nice—because it was different. After a while, it became pleasant enough. Then live-able. Then barely tolerable. And then this morning—I woke up and suddenly felt so completely unhappy. *(Beat)* My whole gut was raging, screaming: "I want to go home".

(Door bell)

HARRY: *(In the distance:)* That's them! Can you get it?!

(ANN goes to the front door and opens it.)

JOHN: Merry ThanksgivingI

ANN: That's not what you say—.

FIONA: *(Over this:)* Look at you! When I was pregnant what I wouldn't have given to look like that!

JOHN: You say—what is it?

SAM: Happy Thanksgiving. Like Happy birthday.

FIONA: Harry's been saying you're getting more beautiful every day.

ANN: Harry's in the garden. Dinner's almost ready.

FIONA: Ann Day—Sam Beach; our token American.

ANN: How do you do?

SAM: How do you do?

ANN: He thought you'd want to have drinks in the garden.

FIONA: It's such a beautiful day. It doesn't seem like November.

JOHN: Sam's been coaching us in the taxi on Thanksgiving etiquette.

SAM: *(As they go through the house:)* I didn't tell you to say "Merry Thanksgiving".

JOHN: He taught us the turkey call, Ann. *(He begins to "gobble".)*

SAM: That's a family thing actually—.

FIONA: *(Over this:)* There's Harry! Harry!

(They hurry into the garden, leaving ANN *alone.)*

ANN: *(To us:)* Two weeks ago, I said to Harry, let's have a Thanksgiving dinner. Let's invite friends. I'll cook! *(Beat)* It was hard for people to take the time off—when it's not a holiday. When it's in the middle of the week. Fiona had a lunch appointment with this—American. So she thought it might be sort of fun. And John's Harry's best friend so… *(Beat)* It seemed a good idea. I thought it would help. It hasn't. I want to go home.

*(*ANN *goes into the garden to join the others. As she approaches:)*

FIONA: The sun feels wonderful.

JOHN: Like summer.

HARRY: It's the global warming. They'll soon be planting palm trees in Hyde Park.

FIONA: *(To* HARRY*:)* Is that a maternity dress? The styles they have now. When I was pregnant—.

HARRY: Sam, do you live in London?

FIONA: He's only visiting—.

SAM: I'm here for a week.

FIONA: We're publishing Sam's novel.

HARRY: So you're a—

FIONA: It's already come out in the States. It's done terribly well.

SAM: No it hasn't.

FIONA: For serious fiction. For the States. *(Beat)* Which means it's sold maybe five copies. *(Laughs)* It'll do very well here we think.

HARRY: When did you arrive?

SAM: Just this morning.

HARRY: You must be jet-lagged. Here, you get the first drink.

SAM: I'm surprisingly awake—. I thought you avoided drinks to get over the—.

HARRY: My method is to think of it all as just one long night.

ANN: *(To us:)* One long night. Made up of days and days. That's how I think of it as well.

HARRY: I should get some more chairs.

ANN: The dinner's nearly ready—.

FIONA: Were we late? If we're late it's my fault.

HARRY: A quick drink.

(Short pause, as HARRY *hands out drinks.)*

HARRY: *(Finally:)* Doesn't Ann look stunning?

FIONA: Fantastic. I've already told—.

JOHN: How many months is it now?

ANN: The baby's due next month.

SAM: A Christmas baby. I was a Christmas baby.

(Pause. Wind blows in the garden.)

SAM: Beautiful garden.

ANN: Harry takes care of it. It's his. If it were up to me I'd just pour cement over the whole thing. It'd be a lot easier. Then we could actually do things on the weekends. *(Beat)* But then—I'm American.

(ANN laughs, then everyone laughs.)

(Short pause)

SAM: I love—all the different flowers.

FIONA: We brought you both a gift. Then in the car, Sam says you don't bring gifts on Thanksgiving. But how did we know. Anyway—it's my fault! *(She laughs.)*

ANN: *(Opening the present:)* Look at this.

FIONA: It's for the garden.

ANN: It's—lovely. I should—check on dinner.

HARRY: *(As she goes:)* My mother had one of these in our garden. I was terribly fond of it.

JOHN: My parents did as well.

ANN: *(To us as she goes:)* I don't even know what it is!

(ANN goes in the house and closes the door behind her.)

ANN: *(As she closes the door:)* It's cold out there. *(She begins to take deep breaths. To us:)* On Thanksgiving morning at home, we watch the parade. Then we play a little touch football. We throw ourselves into piles of leaves. We eat a beautiful dinner, and there's a carved wooden turkey as a centerpiece. All of us kids sit at the card table—so the grownups can talk about what they like. I remember everything. *(She takes a few more deep breaths.)* I'm so tired. *(Beat)* Harry wouldn't even call Fiona and John to ask them. I had to do that. He said why can't we have Thanksgiving on Saturday or

Sunday? He said Thursday was a stupid day to have a holiday. *(Beat)* They came. I told them I needed them. Fiona said she could bring Mr Beach. She said he wasn't an important author, so why not?

SAM: Excuse me.

ANN: *(Startled:)* What?!

SAM: Is the bathroom...?

ANN: Upstairs. First landing. The door on the right.

(SAM *starts to go.*)

ANN: Mr Beach? Where in the States do you come from?

SAM: Philadelphia.

ANN: You must miss it terribly.

SAM: I've only been away—less than a day. First door on the right.

(SAM *goes.*)

ANN: *(To us:)* He reminds me of someone. Who?

FIONA: *(Entering:)* It's colder than you think. Is there anything I can do to help?

ANN: *(To us:)* Who? It's right on the tip of my tongue.

FIONA: When I was pregs I wanted to scream half the time. You look—so together.

ANN: *(To us:)* I know! Seth Miller. Seth was the first boy I ever—did it with. *(Laughs to herself)*

FIONA: Of course I had mine in the summer. You've planned things much—

ANN: *(To us:)* I don't know what it is. It's not that he looks like him. Different color hair even. They—slouch the same. Maybe that's it. *(Beat)* When was this? We were in my bedroom at home. Seth and me. It was after school. We were doing a science project together. We were a team.

> ANN: Stop, Seth. Do you hear me, stop it! You're going to rip my blouse. Stop.
>
> (ANN *and* SETH *pant.*)
>
> SETH: Can I kiss you?
>
> *(Beat)*
>
> ANN: Okay. Not there! Seth—!!
>
> SETH: Ann, I don't know what you want?!
>
> *(Footsteps in the hall)*
>
> ANN: It's Mother!
>
> *(Door opens.)*
>
> MOTHER: Your father called, Ann. His car won't start at the station. I have to pick him up. There's a roast on. When the timer goes ding, will you take it out.
>
> (MOTHER *sets a timer that begins to tick.*)
>
> (MOTHER *starts to go, then stops.*)
>
> MOTHER: What are you two doing in here with the door closed?
>
> *(Beat)*
>
> ANN: A science experiment.

ANN: I can't believe I said that. *(She laughs.)*

FIONA: Here come the men, they couldn't take the cold either.

> *(The bedroom door closes, the timer continues to tick.)*
>
> ANN: *(Listening to the timer:)* We have forty minutes. What do you want to do?
>
> SETH: I think we should undress each other.

ANN: *(To us:)* He had such a thin body. He was only a boy. I undressed him. I let him undress me.

SETH: You lie down. Tell me if I hurt you.

ANN: *(To us:)* It was Seth's first time as well.

SETH: I think you have to help it in, Ann. Take it and help it in.

ANN: *(To us:)* I did. *(She cries out in pain.)*

SETH: Oh God, you're beautiful.

ANN: Am I? Am I, Seth? Am—?

(Kitchen noise and:)

FIONA: Sam's cute, isn't he? I'm going to have to stop signing up these twenty five year-old novelists. My heart can't take it.

(FIONA laughs. ANN laughs.)

ANN: I know what you mean. *(To us:)* Where was I? "Am I, Seth?" "Am I?" Where'd you go, Seth?

(Kitchen noise for a moment, then:)

ANN: *(To us:)* That bed, the one in my room, is still there. I still sleep on-it when I go home. Harry finds this incredible. That when he goes to my house he and I have separate beds. He sleeps in my sister's bed. *(Beat)* Of course she's not there. *(Laughs to herself)* My mother sleeps in the bed she was born in. Her grandmother's bed; where mother was born. Where Grandmother died. *(Beat)* I sleep so good when I'm in that bed. My bed. Or in mother's bed. I've always slept great there too.

HARRY: Ann? Ann?

(This gets louder as ANN comes out of her day-dreams.)

HARRY: Ann!

ANN: What?! We should eat, don't you think? Bring everyone inside.

HARRY: Everyone's at the table, Ann. We're waiting for you. Are you alright? Your face is flushed.

ANN: I'm hot. It's the kitchen. Could you be a dear and carry the turkey?

(ANN *and* HARRY *go out of the kitchen into the diningroom where the others are in the middle of conversation. This gets louder as* ANN *gets closer.*)

SAM: Candied sweet potatoes. Peas. Here comes the turkey.

ANN: With dressing!

SAM: It's all here. She's missed nothing.

JOHN: So in America everyone is eating this same thing right now.

SAM: In about five hours. Because of the time difference. Right now, they're in bed. At least on the West—

ANN: *(To us:)* I'm so tired. I want to be in bed.

HARRY: *(He sounds very far away:)* What were we—? Punting! At school, the three of us—. We all went to University together.

SAM: *(Also very distant:)* Even Ann?

HARRY: No. No, she—

(*The others fade out and for a moment we only hear* ANN *taking long deep breaths. Then the other conversation comes back:*)

JOHN: I think we're boring him!

SAM: Please. I'm interested. I've been wanting to ask someone who knew the game.

JOHN: Actually Fiona's the one who really watches cricket.

ANN: *(To us:)* This young man is so polite. I was like him—when I was first here. I listened too.

(A burst of laughter from the table)

ANN: *(To us:)* When I first arrived, they listened to me too. They laughed at my jokes.

(More laughter)

(Beat)

ANN: What do they see when they look at this table? What does Thanksgiving mean to them? What could it mean? I don't even think we said a prayer. At home Mother always said the prayer; she makes us kids holds hands and bow our heads and she says the prayer. Every year. That was—comforting. You knew what to expect. You knew—where you were.

FIONA: *(She too seems far away:)* Ann? It's absolutely delicious.

SAM: *(Far away:)* Try the cranberries. Take a bite of the turkey with some cranberries.

ANN: *(To us:)* I have grown to hate English people. What they talk about. Their—attitudes toward—everybody else. And what they talk about over and over and over again. It'll be their gardens before too long.

FIONA: When I was eight months pregnant, even the idea of cooking a meal was preposterous. Do you remember, John? I don't know how she does it.

JOHN: She used to lay on a wicker chair in the garden and make me wait on her, even move her—like the beached whale she resembled.

(Laughter)

FIONA: It's when I first learned to appreciate our garden.

ANN: *(To us:)* There. What did I tell you? It's either gardens or—where are you going on your holiday. Or, depending on the time of year—where you went on holiday. They'll get to that too in a minute. "What bloody package tour are you taking this bloody year?!" *(Beat)* When we were kids, Dad'd just throw us in the back seat of our car, warn us not to beat up on each other or else, and then we'd head West—for three days. Or East. Or South. Depended on the year. Three days, we'd see how far we'd get, then turn around and drive home. *(Beat)* That way—we'd get to see our country. Father said. See what's in your blood, what speaks to your soul, what makes you who you are. *(Beat)* Three days—in one direction. The country's that big. You never have to leave these shores. Dad said. It's all here. *(Takes a deep breath)* I keep thinking I'm falling asleep. What's—? Why is it suddenly quiet? Why isn't anyone talking?

(The sound of everyone eating)

ANN: *(To the others:)* Is anything the matter?

JOHN: No, Ann. Everything's delicious.

ANN: No one was saying anything.

JOHN: I suppose an angel passed.

(They eat.)

ANN: *(She thinks she's talking to the others:)* This morning, when I felt an emptiness in my gut, my first thought was—the baby is dead. I knew it had to be dead. I just cried. Didn't I, Harry?

FIONA: You know who else is pregnant? Shiela.

JOHN: In accounting?

THE AMERICAN WIFE

FIONA: Tom's teacher. I don't know what the school's going to do.

JOHN: I was going to say—Shiela in accounting,

ANN: *(Continuing with her story, amazed that no one is reacting:)* Then—the baby kicked. So… But then, I thought it has the cord around its throat and its choking. It's suffocating in me! It's kicking me to get help. It's struggling to breathe. It's thrashing around. It's not dead yet but it's dying!

(Beat)

(They continue to eat:)

HARRY: Sarah had twins.

FIONA: I heard that.

HARRY: *(Over this:)* And she can't wait to come back to work. She says she's never felt more inadequate.

FIONA: They're her first? Who doesn't?

HARRY: Someone was telling us about a couple -who was telling us Ann? They've just had a baby. They leave the hospital, wave goodbye to the head nurse, whose been very kind and supportive, and who shouts back: "Enjoy your baby!" They drive the five minutes home. As they're getting into the house—fiddling for keys, he hands the baby to her, then she to him, then—and they drop it. It cries and cries and they rush it right back to the same hospital, to the same nurse, holding out the child and saying, "we dropped him." They'd had the baby for ten minutes!

(Laughter)

HARRY: Of course the baby was fine.

SAM: When I was ten days old, I'm told—my Aunt came to visit. She took one look at me, squealed with delight, "Oh he's so cute," picked me up under my arms and thrust me up into the air—and right into a low beam in the ceiling. I'm told, she'd thought she'd killed me. *(Beat)* My parents wouldn't let her touch me again until I was seven. And for at least the next fifteen years, whenever she saw me—I could tell she was guiltily looking for any sign of retardation.

(Laughter)

JOHN: The worst child story I know—.

FIONA: *(Interrupting:)* Oh God, don't tell them that!

JOHN: It's funny—.

FIONA: We're eating. They don't want—

HARRY: Tell us. Come on.

(Beat)

JOHN: A friend of mine is traveling in a plane with her year and a half year old son. He is quite a handful, as they say. She's in her seat; he climbs into the aisle, wearing only his nappy. Which he suddenly rips off—it's full of poop of course and as he runs down the aisle he begins to fling that nappy over his head.

HARRY: In the aisle of a plane?

JOHN: Yes.

HARRY: During a flight?

JOHN: A fully-booked flight.

(HARRY groans and they burst out laughing.)

(Over the laughter as it fades:)

JOHN: My friend can't tell that story without breaking into a cold…

(ANN begins to breathe deeply again. the sound of the diningroom comes back, but in the distance.)

FIONA: Are you alright, Ann?

(Phone rings.)

THE AMERICAN WIFE

HARRY: Excuse me.

(HARRY *gets up and leaves the room to get the phone.*)

FIONA: *(A little louder:)* Are you alright, Ann?

ANN: I'm fine.

(*Phone continues to ring, then stops as it is picked up.*)

JOHN: *(Hardly audible:)* What were we talking about? Canal boats! It's not something most tourists would know anything about...

ANN: *(To us:)* That must be her on the phone. His girlfriend. He'd deny it, sure. But we'll see by the way Harry comes back into the room. If he's rubbing his chin—it was her.

FIONA: *(In the distance:)* For some reason, John always thinks of himself as the captain of the ship...

ANN: *(To us:)* I haven't met her myself, of course. Even as of last night, he was still denying she existed. Then I showed him the letter—

(*A burst of distant laughter from around the table*)

ANN: *(To us:)* —I found in the bottom of his briefcase. I remember the whole thing : "Dear Bunny", —I've never called him anything but Harry. "Dear Bunny. I want you. I want to touch you. I want to take off my clothes and jump on you. I want to run my tongue across your thighs. I want to jump naked on your lap, so our wet skins will go smack-smack-smack." *(Beat)* Something like that, I don't remember the exact words, but that was the sentiment, I promise you. So I tell him this and he says that he gets such letters all the time. They're from actresses who wish to work in one of the shows he's producing. And—this is the kicker—the only reason he saved this letter was he thought it so ridiculous it made him laugh and he wanted to show it to me. *(Beat)* To make me laugh. *(Beat)* Ha. Ha. Ha.

I say to him. He says back, that he has never touched another woman since we were married. *(Beat)* What about just before we were married, I ask—we'd lived together for about six months before—. And he says, even then, though he hesitated so I could see he had to think about it. Maybe trying to remember what he'd already confessed to, I don't know. *(Beat)* I say, fine. I kiss him, he smiles and kisses me back then starts to go back downstairs to make—what I'm sure he now believes is a well-earned drink. But I stop him with: "How come there were ten condoms in your top bureau drawer and now there are only two?" *(Beat)* He looks at me, there's fear I think now in his eyes, and he says:

HARRY: Ann, you're eight months pregnant!

ANN: And that makes it all right?!!

HARRY: I mean—you're emotional. You're not seeing things as they really are. I love you. I have never loved you more than I do now. I would never do anything to hurt you. Don't you know that?

ANN: Fine, I say this again. He again kisses me—on the top of my head this time, he shakes his head and smiles and begins to whistle as he leaves the bedroom headed for that longed-for drink.

ANN: One more question, Harry. This morning you left the house wearing blue socks. Now you're wearing brown.

HARRY: You must be mistaken. Why would I change my socks?

ANN: Also—this morning while you were taking a shower, I wrote a small letter "A" —for "Ann", not for—the other—on the elastic of your underpants. May I see if you're still wearing the same pair?

THE AMERICAN WIFE

HARRY: Ann, I don't believe you're doing this. What is wrong with you? Get ahold of yourself!

ANN: *(Over this:)* Let me see your underpants!!!

ANN: *(To us:)* Of course he wouldn't show them to me. Wait. *(Beat)* Here he comes back from the phone. *(Beat)* Scratching his chin. The bastard.

JOHN: *(In the distance:)* The Office. You forget everyone else is working today. What are you talking—.

ANN: *(To us:)* I can hear the conversation he's just had:

GIRLFRIEND: Do you know what I'm wearing. Bunny? Nothing. Nada. Let me run this cordless telephone along my naked breasts. *(She smacks her lips.)* Hear that. Guess what those lips are thinking about? Smack-smack-smack.

ANN: Something like that. *(Beat)* And there he sits—the bastard. As if he's done nothing. *(Beat)* Why is that young man, what's-his-name looking at me? The one who doesn't look like Seth. He's looking right at me. Give me a month, young man. Unburden myself, get my figure back. Then we can talk. *(Beat)* Behind our house in Illinois. Among the pine trees; the grounds so very soft there. I can close my eyes and remember how it feels—the soft needles under me, cushioning me. I'd take you there, young man. *(She laughs to herself:)* What would Harry think about that! How would he like it?

HARRY: *(In the far distance:)* Ann? Ann? Ann?

ANN: Is someone...? Everyone is staring at me. Why? Have I—?

HARRY: *(Louder:)* Ann?

ANN: *(Shutting out the table noise:)* Back to last night. Harry wouldn't let me see his underpants. No way. But I got up in the middle of the night and checked— there was no "A". And I'd used a laundry pen so it couldn't have rubbed off. No, he'd changed—during the day. Why? *(Beat)* Maybe, I thought, he spilled coffee in his lap. But then I noticed he hadn't changed his pants. Maybe, I thought, he'd spilled coffee in his lap, but he'd accidently had his fly open so only his underpants got soaked. *(Beat)* That's possible. *(Beat)* Maybe he played tennis and got them all sweaty. Too bad he doesn't play tennis. *(Beat)* Maybe his girlfriend accidently ripped them while biting them off. *(Beat)* I know which has my vote. *(Short pause)* So—in the morning he wouldn't or couldn't explain my discovery. I told him to call up his friends and tell them I wasn't making any Thanksgiving dinner. *(Beat)* That's when he really got angry.

> HARRY: You invited them! They've already gone to a hell of a lot of trouble to come! They've taken half of bloody day off work! Why? Because they're doing it for you, Ann! They're doing you a bloody favor!!!
>
> ANN: Fine! Fine, let them come! But don't be surprised if suddenly without warning I grab the sweet-potatoes and shove them into your face!!!

HARRY: *(Distant:)* Ann? Ann?

ANN: What??? I'm sorry I was thinking about the... Uh. What???

HARRY: Seth here is thinking of moving to England. One of the reasons he's here is to check out flats.

ANN: *(To us:)* Did he say 'Seth'?

SAM: Only for a year, just to get some distance on—

FIONA: *(Over this:)* There are tons and tons of Americans in London.

JOHN: *(Over this:)* It can't be so different.

FIONA: *(Over this:)* John spent, what was it—ten months?

JOHN: I was in Boston on a film. I love it. Everyone was friendly.

HARRY: But Ann's the one you should talk to. You've adapted pretty well I'd have thought.

JOHN: *(To* SAM*:)* Do you know Cape Cod well?

SAM: A little.

JOHN: There's a village near—.

ANN: *(To us:)* That's just what this country needs—another American. Well, he can have my spot. My seat on this sinking ship. I'm going home.

FIONA: When, Ann?

ANN: *(To us:)* I said that out loud.

HARRY: Once the baby is born. To show him off, of course. Grandparents, Uncles—that sort of thing.

ANN: *(To us:)* Old boyfriends—that sort of thing.

FIONA: How about these plates, Ann?

ANN: What?

FIONA: For the pumpkin pie? Are these the plates you want us to use?

ANN: Let me—

FIONA: Sit, please. You've done enough.

ANN: *(Clears her throat:)* Now that we've brought up the subject—I might as well tell you all that I was thinking about going back—home—for good. *(Beat)* We're separating, Harry and me. Our marriage has been a terrible mistake. I realize that now. But we plan to be very civilized about the whole thing, don't we?

JOHN: What holidays do we have? Bank holiday Monday. It's like we're too embarrassed to celebrate anything.

ANN: *(To us:)* Did I say any of that?

FIONA: You know what's fascinating about this whole tradition is that I thought you Americans killed the Indians.

ANN: *(To us:)* How come when I finally speak my mind no one seems to hear me? *(Yells:)* I'm not speaking a bloody foreign language!!!

SAM: They have gambling now. On their reservations.

ANN: I'm leaving Harry!!!

JOHN: What sort of—

SAM: Casinos. They're like mini-Las Vegases. I saw one advertise a special three-day gambling Thanksgiving!

(Laughter)

ANN: I know I said that out loud! I know you can hear me!! He's cheating on me! His pregnant wife!

HARRY: Who wants more coffee? It's still hot.

ANN: *(To us:)* This morning he took me in his arms and said:

    HARRY: I love you more than words can say.

ANN: *(To us)* I don't believe you. You're just trying to shut me up! *(She begins to breathe heavily again.)* Why can't you hear me?!!!

HARRY: Ann?

FIONA: Look at her eyes. Ann!

JOHN: Drink some water!

(Beat)

HARRY: There. She's fine. She's smiling. You had us worried for a second, Ann.

THE AMERICAN WIFE

FIONA: I used to go all hot like that too.

JOHN: What was I saying? I remember: Sam don't overlook South London. Clapham has some nice—.

(Sudden silence)

ANN: *(To us:)* When I was I think seven, my father said he'd give me five dollars if I could learn the names of the States and their capitals. It took me half of one whole summer, but I did. And I don't think I'll ever forget them either. *(Beat)* The capital of North Dakota is Bismark. South Dakota—Pierre. Florida—Tallahassee. Minnesota—Minneapolis. New Jersy. What's New Jersey. I forget! Trenton! Trenton! I remembered.

(Pause)

(Time has passed and the guests are leaving.)

FIONA: *(Calls off:)* I think I left my purse in there as well. *(Then to* ANN:*)* Ann, you are a wizard. To do all this—I never would have had the energy.

SAM: *(To* JOHN:*)* About how much would you say a flat in Clapham might cost?

JOHN: You said you need three rooms.

SAM: Or two.

FIONA: *(Over this:)* I don't think it's fair to leave you with all this.

ANN: *(To us:)* I'm in the kitchen. How did I get here?

HARRY: *(Entering:)* The washing-up is my job! I shall insist that Ann relax, don't worry. I'm not an ogre. *(Laughter)* She's very beautiful, isn't she?

SAM: Thank you for having me. What an enjoyable first day in London.

HARRY: I think I hear your cab.

FIONA: *(Kissing* ANN:*)* Goodbye dear. Now relax.

JOHN: What a treat and in the middle of the week!

(They are gone.)

ANN: *(To us:)* Oh God! The capital of Minnesota isn't Minneapolis! It's Saint Paul. *(She breathes deeply.)*

(HARRY returns:)

HARRY: Well, I think we've just begun our own tradition! They'll come back next year, I'm sure. Everyone had a wonderful time. *(He kisses her on the cheek.)* You look tired. I'm not surprised. I have to call the office. Promise me, you won't touch the washing up.

(HARRY goes.)

ANN: The capital of Texas is Austin. The capital of New York is Albany. *(Beat)* I know who he's gone to call. Whose voice he needs to hear. *(Beat)* There's the extension right there.

(ANN picks up the phone extention and listens:)

> GIRLFRIEND: *(Over the phone:)* —but I also got you—and I love this—drawers to match.
>
> HARRY: To match the tie? With bunnies? *(He laughs.)*
>
> GIRLFRIEND: With a whole lot of bunnies mating, Harry. It's a real giggle. There's this novelty shop on Charing Cross Road. You should go there with me sometime. They have all kinds of things to try. They had a—
>
> HARRY: *(Interrupting:)* Hello? I think there's someone on the line. Hello? Ann? Is that you? Ann—?

(ANN hangs up.)

ANN: *(To us:)* The capital of Rhode Island—is Providence. *(Beat)* I just remembered a dream I had last night. I dreamed my child and I were taking a trip together. Just us. Her and me. We were climbing mountains in the West. The sky was so blue, her face was so young and happy. And then she slipped and she started to fall but I was able to reach down and grab her hand. I was the only thing keeping her from death.

HARRY: *(His voice barely heard:)* Ann? Was that you on the extension? Look at me, Ann!

ANN: *(To us:)* There she was dangling over the side of a cliff, my hand on her wrist. She was heavy. I tried to pull her in.

HARRY: Ann, I was talking to my office. My office!

ANN: *(To us:)* But somehow I found a reserve of strength I never knew I had and I pulled my child to safety. I saved her.

HARRY: That was my secretary! Mrs Richards! You know her! What is wrong you with you?!!!

ANN: *(To us:)* I saved her. I found the strength to save her.

HARRY: Ann!!!!!

(Silence)

END OF PLAY

www.ingramcontent.com/pod-product-compliance
Lightning Source LLC
Chambersburg PA
CBHW070756100426
42742CB00012B/2158